The Eden Conspiracy

Educating for Accomplished Citizenship

by Joe Harless

with Introduction and Epilogue by
Carl Binder

CAMBRIDGE CENTER FOR BEHAVIORAL STUDIES
LITTLETON, MA

ISBN 978-1-881317-18-0

Published by Cambridge Center for Behavioral Studies™.
550 Newtown Road, Suite 950, Littleton, MA 01460

The Eden Conspiracy was first published by
Guild V Publications, Wheaton, IL. in 1998
ISBN 0-9665010-0-4
LCCN 98-93020

Preamble

The Eden Conspiracy: Educating for Accomplished Citizenship was written by Joe Harless as a book on educational reform for the general public. Since the first printing, there have been notable applications of the principles outlined in the book in both the United States and abroad.

The Cambridge Center for Behavioral Studies is devoted to advance the scientific study of behavior and its humane application to the solution of practical problems. This CCBS edition of *The Eden Conspiracy* "wraps" the original publication with a special Introduction and Epilogue. The Introduction provides context for the book and places it into the lineage of behavioral science that began with B.F. Skinner. The Epilogue documents ongoing real-world application of the principles laid out in *The Eden Conspiracy* and summarizes some of the most important areas of impact to date.

Table of Contents

Introduction to the
Cambridge Center for Behavioral Studies Edition
by Carl Binder
Fall 2016

This is an important book, and Joe Harless, who left us in 2012, was a very good man. Harless was my friend, mentor, and fellow conspirator in the advancement of accomplishment-based performance improvement, and it is an honor to write this introduction to a new edition of *The Eden Conspiracy*. I hope to persuade you that this book is a potential game-changer for evidence-based educational reform. Dr. Harless was a thought leader in the application of behavior science to performance engineering, also known as human performance technology (HPT). Prior to the emergence of HPT, he contributed to instructional design, promoting the value of performance analysis as a precursor to design and development (Harless, 1970). Like other pioneers, including his mentor and colleague, Tom Gilbert (Gilbert, 1978), Joe was committed to the "Educational Revolution" that so many applied behavior scientists have envisioned. He wanted to make a difference–a very *big* difference in how we learn and become accomplished citizens.

Joe was from the deep South, and very proud of it. In college he tried out with the University of Alabama Crimson Tide football team, led by the renowned Coach "Bear" Bryant. He didn't make the team, but accepted the Coach's request to help players keep up their grades so they could stay on the team. He told a lot of good stories about Coach Bryant and his approach to performance. (One of his stories recounted how Bryant once said, in response to a question about motivation, that "I don't motivate 'em. I teach those boys how to win.") Joe always told me that a consultant should have a "shtick." He said that his shtick was "good ol' boy," and that mine was "boy scientist." He was a good ol' boy in the best of ways. Friendly, hospitable, gracious, but also capable of gut-splitting humor among friends, Joe was of average stature, but sometimes seemed larger than life.

When I recently visited Newnan, Joe's long-time hometown in Coweta County, Georgia, to prepare for writing this Introduction and the Epilogue, I met students, faculty, community stakeholders, and Georgia's Lieutenant Governor to learn about the Central Educational Center, an educational program and model that Harless helped to create. I spent an evening barbecue with a group of community leaders, business people, educators, politicians, and other community members.Almost everyone seemed to have known Joe, and many had participated as stakeholders in his local educational reform efforts. I met two young men around 40 years of age whom Joe had coached in soccer. He never claimed to be an athlete, nor had he coached soccer before. But when his young son wanted to play, Joe volunteered to coach. Each of the former players told me, in separate conversations, that while the members of their teams did not have the experience and finesse of players on some of the regional powerhouse teams, Joe's teams often beat the others because he taught them winning strategies and tactics sufficient to outsmart the stronger players. He also coached baseball, teaching his son to bat .500. And the first grade football team Joe coached finished the season unbeaten, un-tied, and unscored-upon. Joe knew how to create conditions for successful performance because he was a masterful applied behavior scientist and a persuasive relationship-builder.

After studying with Tom Gilbert in college, Joe followed Gilbert to a company preparing self-instructional materials, and later to the Centers for Disease Control and Prevention, where they and their colleagues were refining instructional technology. Joe was a leader in the transition from instructional technology to a more systemic approach called *performance* technology. Harless and Gilbert were pioneers in adopting a holistic view of the factors that influence behavior, including but not limited to effective instruction. Both Harless and Gilbert later told stories about their realization that in many situations, a good job aid (checklist, menu, procedure document, etc.) can accelerate performance more rapidly, and at lower cost, than training. Joe later created a systematic approach for deciding when to use a job aid, then designing and testing job aids to produce big jump-ups in human performance. His JAWS (Job Aids Workshop) program taught thousands of people in organizations to produce reliable improvements in performance using job aids.

Joe created the term *front-end analysis* to describe a systematic problem-solving investigation that should occur prior to designing any performance improvement effort, extending well beyond the conventional needs analysis that instructional designers typically conduct. His 1970 book, *An Ounce of Analysis,* laid a foundation for many current-day performance improvement methodologies. After years of leading a consulting firm which conducted large projects for client organizations and established in-house capabilities for organizations desirous of using performance problem solving to winnow out the most cost effective times to use training, Joe, "the trainer's trainer," transitioned to teaching and mentoring others in his FEA (Front-End Analysis) program and Job Aids Workshop (JAWS). His most comprehensive contribution, was the ABCD System–*Accomplishment-Based Curriculum Development.* As you will read later in this volume, ABCD set the stage for his approach to educational planning and curriculum design.

Links to Behavior Science

Harless sits squarely in the lineage of B.F. Skinner. He first met Skinner and Dr. Sue Markle, an early Skinner PhD who was a pioneer in instructional design, when he gave his first presentation at the annual conference of the National Society for Programmed Instruction (NSPI) in 1963. Tom Gilbert, his original mentor, did postdoctoral work with Skinner at the Office of Programmed Instruction. Joe paid close attention to the literature of behavior science, and was among the most important thought leaders and a President of what began as the National Society for Programmed Instruction and became the International Society for Performance Improvement (ISPI).

When I met Joe in the mid 1980's, he was a rock star at ISPI, a thought leader and charismatic proponent of systematic, accomplishment-based performance improvement. He was always learning, even from junior colleagues, including me. He graciously told me after he retired that if he had done another edition of his programs, he would have included what he learned from me about behavioral fluency (www.fluency.org) as part of his methodology.

Joe followed Tom Gilbert's (1978) critique of "the cult of behavior," pointing out that the *value* of performance is in the products of behavior, what Gilbert first called *accomplishments*, not in behavior itself, which is costly to establish and support. (As Ogden Lindsley often pointed out, even in a behavior scientist's animal laboratory, the switch-closure that releases food is the valuable accomplishment of the animal's behavior.) By focusing on the accomplishments of an individual, a team, a process, or an organization, Harless connected performance of people with the needs and wants of stakeholders, to whom the accomplishments are delivered. This insight has far-reaching implications, and Harless clarified them. As you will see in this book, he envisioned a seamless educational system for producing truly *accomplished citizens*–people able to achieve what they need to succeed in society. His extension of accomplishment-based performance improvement into education has implications for working with the stakeholders in a community to define desired student accomplishments, and to design educational curriculum enabling students to achieve those accomplishments.

A focus on accomplishments in program design can increase both instructional efficiency and learner engagement. Beginning an instructional sequence with the expectation that, "At the end of this program you will be able to *produce* the following valuable accomplishments for your work or your life" is an attention-grabber. This contrasts with more traditional behavioral objectives, stated as, "At the end of this program you will be able to *behave* in the following ways." Accomplishments define the *value* that behavior contributes by describing what is produced when the behavior is successful. Instructional designers can identify behavior needed to produce those accomplishments, as well as the specific skills and knowledge required for that behavior, more easily than when they are given descriptions of the behavior or skills without clear specification of the valuable accomplishments that behavior will produce.

When   learners   know   that   their   behavior   produces accomplishments that contribute to the greater good (organizational or societal results), they often find more *purpose* in their work. When we focus on valuable accomplishments, we may also identify natural motivating consequences for people, connecting learners more directly to so-called intrinsic motivation. As a colleague of mine in the U.K. once said after hearing about an accomplishment-based approach, "You're talking about what the organization needs from its people!" We might also describe the accomplishments that a *society* needs from its people for them, and the society at large, to be successful.

What Is the Purpose of Education?

For several years before and after retiring from his corporate performance improvement business, Joe asked people whom he encountered, "What is the purpose of education?" That question prompted descriptions of *accomplishments* that citizens must produce to be successful. He created lists of accomplishments such as *an informed reproductive decision, a balanced bank account, a good job, a successful marriage, a driver's license,* and so on. Such lists, like those in chapter 8 of this book, illustrate how an accomplishment-based approach can be clarifying, and potentially comprehensive. While it would be virtually impossible to identify *all the behavior* people need for success, we can certainly list the *most important accomplishments* that determine success in life and employment. Such lists of accomplishments allow curriculum designers to organize and align behavior, skills, and knowledge with the accomplishments they are intended to produce. Identifying what Harless called *behavioral processes* follows relatively easily from identification of needed accomplishments.

Seamless Life-Long Education

Harless pushed back on the idea that curricula can be usefully organized by topics or areas of subject matter. Instead, we should design our curricula and our teaching methods so that learners can reliably produce valuable accomplishments. Harless argued that education and development should occur across a *seamless* environment of instruction, life experience, work experience, mentoring, and practice. It should all work together toward a common purpose. Full realization of this vision, he argued, will require a "conspiracy" among all stakeholders in any given community.

Not Just a Vision

You will read in the Epilogue about what has evolved from Harless's vision in the nearly 20 years since he wrote this book. The "mother program" at the Central Educational Center (CEC) in Newnan, Georgia, and its more than 36 replications in other parts of Georgia, elsewhere in the United States, and extending around the world, have produced remarkable results, some of which become more obvious when you see, as I did, confident teenagers achieving professional-level accomplishments, and loving it. It was quite a contrast to see bright-eyed high school students at CEC compared with the many bored and cynical students I have seen in typical high schools over the years.

This book proposes that parents, educators, business people, and policy makers adopt both a commonsense and a technically superior approach to stakeholder-driven educational reform. This *Introduction* is a call to my colleagues in the Learning Sciences branch of our field (what Harless called *Instructional Science*) to integrate an accomplishment-based approach with effective instructional methods. Harless's methodology offers guiding principles that can be wedded to evidence-based instructional methods that other behavior scientists have created and refined. An accomplishment-based curriculum design aligned with the needs and wants of local stakeholders (bottom-up vs. top-down), implemented with measurably superior instructional procedures, offers an enormous opportunity for expanding human capability in ways that we cannot fully appreciate now.

Joe's vision went beyond the design of "career academies"– the label given CEC and its replications. He encouraged us to extend the accomplishment-based approach based on stakeholder analysis and engagement beyond career and professional development to personal, social, and even cultural development, focused on valuable accomplishments that every person needs to be a successful participant in the community. Pre-school, elementary and middle school, as well as continuing adult education would be parts of the seamless system, designed to precede and to follow the high-school/college hybrid embodied in CEC.

Bottom-Up vs. Top-Down Educational Reform

One of Harless's greatest discoveries is that educational reform has a greater chance of success if it can be driven bottom-up, not top-down. This does not mean we should leave curriculum to whatever people in a particular school system, region, or state prefer. Rather, we should involve all stakeholders in our communities to define the *accomplishments* and *key behavior* that the children and adults in those communities need to be successful. In Coweta County, Georgia, Harless engaged literally hundreds of stakeholders–citizens from all walks of life–in a process of front-end analysis to decide as a community what their children and young adults needed to achieve. Much of the analysis focused on the needs of the local economy, on how high paying jobs could be attracted to Coweta County, and how young people could be prepared to succeed and thrive in those jobs. It also focused on "work ethic" and how an adult behaves in civil society. It engaged everyone in defining career options for their children that would meet the needs of employers in the community, options like being a filmmaker, a robotics designer, a dental assistant, a welder, or a manufacturing engineer. When young people can see that their learning will enable them to become accomplished in ways that they care about–well, you should see the light in those young people's eyes!

I, and many of my colleagues in Precision Teaching (PT), Direct Instruction (DI), the Personalized System of Instruction (PSI), and other educational applications of behavior science, attempted for years to engage school systems, state education departments, and the Federal Government in a process of defining exemplary methods and curricula, and then driving them "down" into schools from above. We learned from hard experience that this might work for awhile, but when the sponsors move on, it seldom sustains itself. In my view, top-down educational reform simply does not work, and Joe Harless articulated a viable and very powerful alternative.

The roots of a top-down approach are not deep enough for long-term survival. Harless's approach identified the accomplishments and key behavior that stakeholders in the community sought in those who come of age in their community. With curriculum grounded in such an accomplishment-based stakeholder-aligned foundation, virtually all members of the community, the economy of the community, its politics, and its civic improvement become both drivers of and roots for sustainment. There is a general, tangible sense of "ownership" by all stakeholders that makes all the difference.

The Epilogue provides additional details, but let it be said here: Harless might have cracked the nut of sustainment when it comes to educational reform by showing that it must be built on the valuable accomplishments needed by a local community. These accomplishments are likely different from what might be needed in another community, in both big and small ways, even a community in the same region but with a different economic, cultural, and political context. Adaptation to these differences, it appears, may determine the long-term viability of any educational program or system.

Dear Reader

Let me add one bit of advice to you. This book is a combination of ambitious vision and methodological detail. It is precise and measured, but also philosophical. It has the potential for engaging many different audiences, although the intended audience is educators, policy makers, and the immediate stakeholders of our educational systems. The ideas in this book are big; so don't let them get lost in the details. And, if the vision and potential of this approach grab you in the same way that they have grabbed me and thousands of other readers and stakeholders, pass this book on to your educators and elected officials. This book, combined with your outspoken support, could make an enormous positive impact on our educational systems and programs.

References

Gilbert, T.F. (1978). *Human Competence: Engineering Worthy Performance.*

Harless, J.H. (1970). *An Ounce of Analysis.* Newnan, GA: Guild V. Publications.

www.fluency.org. The web site of The Fluency Project, Inc., containing downloadable articles and other documents about the scientific origins and application of fluency-based instruction.

Publisher's Note

The Cambridge Center is proud to have a role in reprinting and distributing *The Eden Conspiracy*. It describes a unique and highly successful approach to educational innovation that should be read by all who would seek to improve the quality of American public education. The author, the late Joe Harless, is well known in the field of Performance Improvement for his Accomplishment-Based Curriculum Development System. This approach shifts the emphasis in setting performance objectives from behavior to the valuable accomplishments produced by the learner's behavior. Such objectives define the products of behavior, not the behavior itself. A unique feature of Harless's application of this concept to a public school system is that the citizens of the town determine the accomplishments that the system should engender. Subject matter becomes secondary to these objectives but becomes instrumental in achieving them. All participants—teachers, parents, citizens, politicians—act in a unified manner to implement the system.

Originally launched by a county school system in Georgia, this model quickly spread throughout the state and has been supported by politicians at the highest level as well as foundations and other funding organizations. Supplemental material included in this republication describes this growth in detail. The sustained success of Harless's model should serve to encourage all who share our commitment to the application of our science to the betterment of our culture.

We wish to thank our trustee, Carl Binder, not only for bringing *The Eden Conspiracy* to our attention, but for his leadership in seeing this project to fruition. He has thereby made a contribution in total harmony with the mission of the Cambridge Center.

Henry S. Pennypacker
Board Chair, CCBS

The Eden Conspiracy

Educating for Accomplished Citizenship

 by Joe Harless

Acknowledgments

If I were to acknowledge all the people who have influenced the ideas in this book, the listing would exceed the contents of the volume itself. There is, however, a more finite number to whom I owe special thanks (or perhaps blame)…

Tom Gilbert, an early mentor, who showed me that teaching could be approached as a science; and, who taught me to concentrate on outputs before considering processes; and, who was a model for the idea that we make progress when we challenge current paradigms, despite the slings and arrows that are sure to follow.

Roger Kaufman, who convinced me that educational design must take place in context of societal design.

Carl Binder, who was relentless in his insistence I include exercises in my instructional process that ensure the student will be fluent in the learning; and, who showed me how to do that.

Bob Mager (who perhaps influenced more people than all of us in the field added together), who blazed the trail for wider dissemination of the techniques practiced by a small "cult"; and, who formulated many of them himself.

Steven Lee Harless, Carol Pulliam Harless, Tony Moore, Paul Elliott, and Claude Lineberry, who took time away from their careers to help with this book; and, offered encouragement when I dallied or flirted with cynicism.

The hundreds of stakeholders in education across the country who responded to my surveys concerning curriculum content; and, who confirmed I was not alone in my concern for education.

About the Author

For more than 30 years Joe Harless headed the Harless Performance Guild, a network of organizations and consultants who use his concepts and procedures to help business, industry, and the military improve the performance of their employees. He is generally recognized as one of the founders of the relatively new field of Human Performance Technology.

He is the author of the acclaimed *Accomplishment-Based Curriculum Development System* (ABCD), that has been installed in the educational departments of numerous organizations in the U.S. and Canada. The *ABCD System* is widely regarded as state-of-the-art in instructional development.

His most recent writing, the *Peak Performance System*, is a massive work that provides detailed guidelines for analysis, design, and development of a wide range of interventions to improve people-performance.

Harless received the *Gilbert Distinguished Professional Achievement* award from the International Society for Performance Improvement in 1996, and was elected to the Human Resources Development Hall of Fame in 1988.

Recently retired from active management of his company, Harless now devotes his time to reflection and research. *The Eden Conspiracy* is the first of a series of commentaries on societal problems and needs.

Contents

I. The Author's Presumptions

This book is presumptuous. Perhaps its author is also arrogant to claim the radical shift in education proposed herin would be superior ...

...to the numerous attempts to redesign education in the last 50 years. This book is presumptuous because it calls into question the traditional purpose and ostensible goals of education held by most educators, and even most educational reformers. This book challenges the convention that it is the state and the educational institutions which should decide the *content* of the K-12 curriculum. It is also presumptuous because it outlines a methodology for instruction our teachers were not taught in schools of education in college, but stems from research and experience outside the mainstream of public education.

There is some justification for these presumptions. The need for educational reform is now generally acknowledged by both our political leaders and the grass-roots citizenry. Also, attempts in the last decade, and those currently proposed, do not attack the fundamental causes of the problems in public education. Thus, many of the solutions being suggested now are likely to suffer the same fate as most educational reform interventions always have: *high expenditure, low return.*

As the author of these presumptions, I might well be considered arrogant because this book suggests an approach that is fundamentally different from those that always have been followed by formal education. It proceeds from a different base and assumption. This book outlines a procedure for deriving WHAT should be taught. The derivation of content procedure proposed progresses from a different base than is traditional. I call this foundation an *accomplishment-base,* which is in contrast to the traditional foundation for education—*subject-matter* groupings of knowledge in general categories such as history, chemistry, math and so forth.

This book also provides a sketch for HOW to teach. The approach outlined is a direct and precise methodology for the design and delivery of accomplishment-based content. It is more akin to engineering than art. I call this methodology *Instructional Science.*

What qualifies me to challenge the educational establishment? I have never taught below the graduate school level. I have not been a school principal or served on a board of education. Until doing the data collection for this book, I have dealt with public schools only in the capacities of student, parent, and an infrequent volunteer provider of in-service seminars for faculties. Is it therefore presumptuous of me to criticize public education? On what basis could one justify the arrogance of suggesting fundamental changes in what and how to teach the young?

I have good credentials to do so: I am a citizen of a democratic society, and take seriously the right to speak for/against public institutions; my tax dollars contribute to the funding of public education; I am a parent, and in that sense, the advocate for every child; and, perhaps most qualifying, I am a receiver and a customer of the public education process in my roles as potential employer and member of the community. I must hire and live with the "product" of public education. That is, I am, as we all are, a STAKEHOLDER in public education. As a stakeholder, I feel no hesitancy in speaking out for what I believe to be a better way.

Former Secretary of Education William Bennett in his book *Our Children, Our Country* makes a similar invitation:

> *If the current reform movement is to succeed, it must rest on the conviction that the public schools belong to the public, not to the experts, or social scientists or professionals, or the educational establishment.*

If it is arrogant to offer different paradigms for what and how our educational system teaches our young, I can only state my reasons for such immodest behavior. I have spent my entire professional life researching, developing, and teaching the methodologies for influencing people—especially in the domain of influencing their knowledge and skills.

For over 30 years the consulting firm I head has been teaching courses to human resource development professionals on how to systematically analyze, design, and develop instruction. In earlier years some thought us to be radical when we employed a different way to derive instructional content, and for the rigorous methods we employed for instructional design and delivery. What was considered revolutionary in the '70s is becoming somewhat common today in human resources development. Little of this work, however, has found its way into public education. Despite nearly two decades of attempts at educational reform, education progresses in much the same way as it always has in terms of what and how it teaches. The results continue to be disappointing, if not alarming.

Public education is not the same as business/industry education. All the successful methodologies we've employed will not necessarily transfer to education of the young, but many will if they are tailored to fit the K-12 situation. Almost every time we give our courses in instructional development to human resources professionals, some of our students ask why the models and procedures they were learning were not being utilized in public education. Some even mildly chastise me for not having carried our research and development to the public education domain. (It is interesting to note that many attendees to our courses were former public school teachers, now working in human resources development.)

Although our work has been predominantly in the private sector as consultants to human resources development organizations in business, industry, military, and government, some of the methodologies we've developed portend to have substantial application to the schooling of the young in the K-12 years of their lives. The methodologies also have applicability to the college experience, but I've elected to concentrate on the traditional K-12 progression in this commentary.

This book is written for my fellow stakeholders: parents, potential employers, members of local school boards, and the citizenship at large. Though they are certainly stakeholders also, this book was not written with the academician or my fellow learning researchers in mind. This work is based on extensive research, but I have tried not to pen a scholarly treatise. The urge was great, but I have not filled the pages with charts, graphs, and detailed descriptions of the research on learning.

I make no apology for the presumptions herein. I'll live with the possible charge of arrogance. It will not be the academicians and theorists who will precipitate a radical redesign of education. If it happens, it will start with us, the stakeholders, who were so presumptuous.

1. Educational Reform Deja Vu

Legislated and conventional approaches to fixing education seem to ebb and flow like the tides that rush in only to recede and be replaced by another wave ...

–Roger Kaufman
Mapping Educational Success

Whatever the national ill, we seem to lay root-cause to failure to properly educate the young, and call for educational reform. It is almost a knee-jerk response to heap blame on the schools for *societal* problems such as violence, drugs, teen pregnancy, crime, and even bankruptcy. Whatever the problem being discussed in the media, we can anticipate the called-in "expert" will intone an educational solution. This is analogous to a physician responding to every ill with a dose of antibiotics. We don't take the time to perform very much problem diagnosis, but jump to conclusions about root-causes, and throw money at a presumed educational solution. It is seems to be the American way.

In the middle 1950s' poor science education was blamed for our under-accomplishment in space as compared to the USSR. A panicky call went out for educational reform in science. I was taking high school physics when Sputnik shocked America. In my school we were harangued to take more science courses and exhorted to study harder. I didn't see much change in the content or the way science was taught except our teacher threatened us with bad grades and assigned two chapters in the textbook for the week instead of one. We did note our teacher tacked up quotes from Newton and Einstein, and some photos of the planets. I don't know if we learned any more science, but I recall just feeling guilty about somehow being personally responsible for being behind in the Space Race. Society blames the schools. Schools blame the young.

Social-reforming Presidents such as John F. Kennedy and Lyndon B. Johnson caused billions to be pumped into education to combat poverty, lack of equal opportunity, and social injustice. Nicer schools were constructed. More audio-visuals were bought with federal funds. Head Start and *Sesame Street*, to name just two examples, were touted to be key solutions to educational problems. The results continued to decline.

The modern era of increasing crime, violence, drug addiction, teen pregnancy, AIDS, and declining global competitiveness predictably precipitated the current demand for intervention on how the young are educated. President Bush even used the term *Educational Revolution* to sound-bite a clarion call, and deemed himself the *Education President*. President Clinton has been very vocal on the matter. He has caused much activity including sundry conferences, called for national standards for education, and backed legislation for more funding of education to put more computers in the schoolrooms, improve the buildings, nationwide testing and the like. Much attention has been given to governors' conferences on educational reform.

I accept our leadership's concern is genuine and laud their calling attention to the need, but I respectfully submit the state of education is virtually unchanged; I predict current suggestions will not improve the situation dramatically no matter which one or which combination of reforms is funded.

In spite of decades of educational reform, the *content* of curricula is the same in its essence. Students still struggle to memorize facts whose near and long-term relevance seems to them to be known only by the teacher. I suspect if the real truth could be exposed, the teacher would be hard-pressed to defend why so much of this important time in the young citizens' lives should be taken up trying to acquire most of the stuff presented. *Relevance* and *importance* seem not to be relevant variables when deciding what to teach. Teachers tend to teach what they've been taught.

In addition to highly questionable content, teachers by and large still employ the same ineffective teaching and motivational techniques that have always been practiced: *I talk. You listen. You study, I give tests. I sort you into piles of A's, B's, C's, D's, and F's. Here is the next set of facts.* The advent of expensive educational hardware in the classroom and various short-lived instructional fads are trumpeted in the media, but educational quality has not improved very much even when measured by traditional assessments such as standardized tests.

The current iteration of calls for education reform was spurred and galvanized by *A Nation At Risk: The Imperative for Education Reform*, a high-impact report from the National Commission on Excellence in Education in 1983. A few of the Commission's findings:

- On 19 academic tests American students, compared with other industrialized nations, placed *last* seven times. They were never first or second on any of the tests.
- SAT scores had an unbroken decline for the previous 20 years.
- Less than a third of 17 year-olds could solve a math problem requiring several steps. Remedial math courses constituted one-quarter of all math courses taught in public four-year colleges.
- There was a steady decline in science test scores since 1969.
- Nearly 40% of 17 year-olds could not draw inferences from written material.
- One-quarter of the Navy's recruits could not read at the minimum level sufficient to understand safety instructions.

Among the comments in the Commission's report:

We are raising a new generation of Americans that is scientifically and technologically illiterate. More and more young people emerge from high school ready neither for college nor for work.

...the educational foundations of our society are presently being eroded by a rising tide of mediocrity that threatens our very future as a nation and a people.

And perhaps the most quoted comment from *A Nation At Risk*...

If an unfriendly power had attempted to impose on America the mediocre educational performance that exists today, we might well have viewed it as an act of war.

A Nation At Risk and numerous subsequent investigations into the state of education in America precipitated a flood of commissions, books, and TV special reports. An entire new industry of educational reform consultants and companies was created. Numerous reform programs were launched.

Five years after *A Nation At Risk* and other stimuli which caused the flurry of educational reform efforts, the White House conducted a meeting to review and celebrate the accomplishments of the reform programs. Attendees seem to be floored by the general conclusion: **There were none.**

I am not surprised. In spite of doing an excellent job documenting the need for educational reform and alerting the nation to the seriousness of the situation, *A Nation At Risk* merely called for more of the same, as do many current reform suggestions: Teach more of the same subject-matter; increase the length of the school year; give more tests; give more teachers more money. There was no serious questioning of the basic assumed purpose and goals of education. There was little mention of the possible need to revamp WHAT should be taught. Little was said about bringing to educators the now known techniques for improving learning which are currently being embraced with significant impact by American business, industry, and military in their education programs.

In 1990 a report produced by the Educational Testing Service, "The Education Reform Decade," reviewed the 1980s' wholesale attempt at educational improvement. Analysis of results showed little improvement in any area. The report stated:

> *The processes and content of instruction in the public school classrooms of today are little different from what they were in 1980 or 1970.*

Reading the massive outpouring of the educational reform literature, I am struck by the absence of very much systematic problem-analysis as the basis for the interventions (changes) recommended. In fact, the usual commission/book/report/article says: *Education is in trouble. Here is THE solution.* A given reformer usually has a favorite intervention that will "fix" education such as national standards; parental choice of schools; smaller classes; more computers in the classrooms; heterogeneous grouping; tougher graduation requirements; more pay for teachers; pay more teachers; "back-to-basics"; school-business partnerships, longer school year; vouchers, and many more.

One of the difficulties with most of these single-intervention designs for reform is that education suffers from a *complex* of problems. Anyone familiar with the research on problem-solving can tell you that multiple problems usually require multiple solutions. It is rare there is a single magic bullet for any problem, much less for a complex of them. As Chester E. Finn of Vanderbilt University put it in his *We Must Take Charge. Our Schools and Our Future*:

> *The idea of education reform has won tenure. The only thing it hasn't done is palpably improve the skills and knowledge of the average child. Which, of course, is the only important thing it was asked to do.*

We're dealing with a very sick patient in the '90s, and it is prudent to take a full case history before venturing new therapies.

I choose to interpret Professor Finn's comment as agreeing with me: We need to perform systematic diagnosis before prescribing interventions.

The difficulty with most, if not all, educational reform efforts is they do not address in any systematic way the most basic and fundamental front-end questions. I submit the basic issues are:

1. What is the ultimate *purpose* and *goal* of education?
2. What are the student *accomplishments* desired as a result of the educational process?
3. What is the *gap* between current accomplishments and desired accomplishments? What are the *root-causes* of the gap? What *solutions* (interventions) are indicated?
4. What *content* should be taught?
5. How should education be *designed* and *delivered?* How should education be *evaluated?*

Those questions must be addressed in detail *before* embarking on the specific combination of interventions to reduce the gap between what IS and what SHOULD be. And, the issues above should be addressed in that order and no other because the findings of each analytical step impact the next.

An ounce of analysis up-front might be worth a pound of interventions.

Changes always encumber a cost. Some changes are very expensive. We have expended many pounds in attempts to improve education. For instance, the "smaller classes" intervention requires a dramatic increase in expenditure for more teachers, more buildings, more equipment, and more overhead. If so, is it not reasonable that we have some expectation, if not assurance, the increase in expenditure will yield a positive return? If not, it is a foolish gambit.

The "smaller classes" intervention could be a prime example. It almost always is a knee-jerk response by educational reformers and school teachers. Private schools very often advertise this alleged benefit. It seems to be common sense the fewer the number of students the teacher has, the more individual attention he/she will pay to each student, thus the greater the learning. But when the assumption is put to controlled test, the result of smaller student-to-teacher ratio begins to bear significant fruit only when it gets down to about half the current student-teacher ratio now in public schools. Further, the studies seem to show small ratios are not as important much beyond the first three years of school.

In South Korea the typical math class is about 50 students. In the U.S. it is about 23. Yet South Korea's 9 and 13 year-olds outstrip ours on standardized math tests. There are variables in addition to student-teacher ratio which might contribute to the comparative performances, but such does not support the contention of smaller classes per se.

Kentucky's all-out attempt to improve education early in this decade might be illustrative of the kinds of funds that can be spent on reform. The state increased per pupil expenditure 40% from 1990 to 1996. (It spent $136 million on computers alone.) It enacted a $1 billion tax increase to fund various interventions. Review of results and opinions about the reform efforts have been mixed at best. None would term the results "dramatic." Only Kentuckians should say if the returns were worth the expenditure.

Kansas City is another case in point. It poured over $1 billion, I am told, into educational reform—new state-of-the-art buildings, computers in the classrooms, reduction of class sizes and so forth. The results have been meager.

I can't speak for Kentucky and Kansas City, but it seems most attempts at education reform have been gambits that have not yielded comparable returns in terms of student achievement. In fact, it would seem that **there is little correlation between expenditure per se and improvement.**

Reviewing the attempts at educational reform of the last 50 years, it is tempting to say "nothing works so why bother." Many of my colleagues say this. I too descend into cynicism on occasion, but I believe we can and must reform education. But the reforms must be based on a systematic problem diagnosis procedure such as the five-step process outlined above and discussed in subsequent chapters.

2. A Tale of Two Cities

What would work? How could we find out? I have a day-dream of two identical cities who attempted educational reform. If we had such, we could conduct an experiment ...

... concerning the effectiveness of differing approaches to educational reform. Such a situation is, of course, impossible, but a rough "thought experiment" might be instructive.

My two fantasy cities are *Medianville* and *Eden*. They are twin in every respect—same size, same state, have comparable industries and businesses. They are the same in economic, racial, and ethic makeup, and so forth. Eden and Medianville both sought to improve education in their cities, but they took very different approaches to education reform.

Education Improvement in
MEDIANVILLE

In the middle '80s the concerned school board of Medianville conducted a series of meetings and retreats with the superintendent of schools and her staff to the address the question: *What should we do to improve education in Medianville?*

The first effort in the project involved review of the purpose and goals of education in general. They took as a given the fundamental purpose of education is *to teach the subject-matters of math, science, grammar, history, geography, and literature.* In other words, the ultimate objective of education is knowledge of "subject matter."

Little time was spent addressing the issue of WHAT should be taught. As everyone always had, they took as a given that reading, writing, arithmetic, and a little grammar would be taught in the early years. Math, history, science, English, and perhaps a second language would be taught in the upper grades. It didn't occur to the retreatees that someone other than the teachers of the specific subject-matter might have any relevant input to the content of the curriculum.

It was assumed evaluation of content acquisition ("learning") would be left to the teachers in the form of teacher-constructed quizzes and exams, except for state-mandated standardized tests. Not much time was spent in diagnosing the problems and needs of Medianville students. Instead, the group "brainstormed" the interventions below that were intended to improve the quality of education in Medianville:

1. *Increase the salaries of teachers.* The group assumed if the pay were higher, then the better teachers would be retained; and, all teachers would be more motivated to improve their instruction.

2. *Reduce the teacher-student ratio.* If there were smaller classes, then each student would receive more individual attention; and, teachers would be more motivated because of a lightened workload.

3. *Institute a tougher grading policy.* If they raised what constitutes a given letter-grade by two points, this would encourage students to work harder. (They called this raising the standards.)

4. *Group students by ability.* They would sort students based on IQ test given in early grades. It was assumed this would allow teachers to adjust the teaching to the potential of the student—more work for the able student, less demanding work for the less capable.

5. *Provide more audio-visuals.* They equipped classrooms with video-tape playback equipment, overhead projectors, and a computer for each elementary classroom.

6. *Institute a "Teacher of the Year" award.* A tactic intended to motivate the teachers.

7. *Encourage "back-to-basics."* Recommend to elementary teachers to put more effort into teaching the "3 R's."

8. *Form alliances with local businesses.* What this would entail was not specified, but Medianville's employers were always complaining about the students the schools were producing.

The Eden Conspiracy

The interventions above were instituted in Medianville during the mid-'80s and early '90s. Recently, the school board decided to conduct a formal review of the state of education in Medianville. The board employed an independent educational evaluation organization to conduct the analysis. Among the findings of the study concerning academic performance after the interventions above were implemented:

- Virtually no improvement in reading scores in elementary school grades. Reading scores actually declined in high school seniors. (60% judged as "deficient.")
- SAT scores remained virtually flat, no significant improvement.
- 36% of Medianville's high school graduates entering college were required to take one or more remedial courses their first year.
- High school dropout rate remained between 25% and 30%. No significant improvement. There was no significant difference in dropout rate whether student's family was "poor" or not.
- 97% of high school seniors could not write above a minimal or adequate level.
- Of the students who had an "A" average in science courses in high school, very few could solve a basic science problem or answer a basic science question when given the problem/question slightly changed from the form in which it was instructed in class.
- One in three of Medianville's students who took calculus in college dropped or failed the course.
- 25% believed the sun rotates around the earth.
- 50% of high school seniors could not interpret a bus schedule. 15% could not address an envelope.
- Less than 10% of students could compute what a borrower would owe on loan of $850 at 12% interest. 30% could not make change.

- Less than 50% could find New York on a blank map. 75% could not say when Lincoln was President, or in what half of the century the Civil War occurred. 50% did not recognize names of Winston Churchill and Joseph Stalin. 40% did not know Japan bombed Pearl Harbor. 37% could not place WW II in the correct half century.
- Three out of four applicants for entry-level jobs at the largest industry in the area were rejected because they failed to score the minimum on a basic literacy test.
- Local employers continued to voice dissatisfaction over the performance of new hires, citing lack of work ethic and poor entry skills as the most frequent reasons for their concern. Only 23% of the employers surveyed rated the school system "good" or "excellent." (91% of the teachers rated the performance of the schools as good or excellent.) As far as education-business partnerships, many businesses stated they were asked only to contribute money to the schools.
- **This year Medianville spent nearly $6,000 per pupil—about a 50% increase (adjusted for inflation) from the pre-intervention period. The largest share of the increase went to raises in compensation of teachers and for additional teachers required by smaller classes.**

In my daydream I attend the graduation ceremony at one of Medianville's schools. In the audience of the capped and gowned youngsters are parents, relatives, and a few high school teachers. There are no other townspeople.

I try to read the feelings of the graduates from their faces. All seem happy enough. Is it because of a sense of accomplishment? Or is it because they have at last completed their sentences? I can't tell. But I know the data about these young people:

- The incidents of violence in the schools rose dramatically during the period studied. 20% of the students admitted having brought a weapon to school. (This required the Medianville school board to introduce interventions they had not anticipated: metal detectors and guards.)
- Of the teens and young adults who would die, the second most frequent cause would be homicide.
- One in three of the young women in Medianville became pregnant during their teen years, the large majority were unmarried. (This was an increase of more than 200% since 1960.)
- 33% of high school students admitted to use of illegal drugs.
- 33% of middle and high school students missed 10 or more days of school each year.
- Of the students who dropped out of high school, more than half would appear before a judge within five years.
- Of the half who would go on to college, half would not adequately be prepared. Most would not obtain degrees.
- The class valedictorian and salutatorian would continue to make good grades in college, but in five years after receiving their degrees, they would not differ significantly from their fellow college graduates in earnings or position in their organizations.
- Of the half who would seek to enter the work force directly, their employers would say they are deficient in: written communications (94% of employers); basic math skills (92%); oral communications (91%); work with a group (87%); and, basic computer skills (86%).

The Medianville school system cannot, of course, be blamed for all of these problems, but it is clear the *interventions* taken did not help to minimize the academic or social problems very much. There were not many smiles among the school board members. Many had become cynical about improving education in Medianville.

Education Improvement in EDEN

Graduation Day in the City of Eden. Several hundred proud relatives and members of the community viewed the youngsters parade into the high school stadium for the Commencement ceremony. The onlookers knew most of graduates from many years of involvement with the schools in Eden.

Many in the audience did not have a daughter or son in this year's group of graduates. School board members were present, of course, but also the heads of local industries and businesses, a Congresswoman, caseworkers from children services organizations, the Sheriff, the entire city council, religious leaders, and heads of local labor unions.

In Eden the schools are the focal points for a wide variety of societal functions in addition to places where young people acquire skills and knowledge (and perhaps attitudes) to be successful in society. Edenites believe school and society should be **seamless.** They appreciate the most important period in the child's life is *before* they are school age. All the children get a "head start" from early-learning programs delivered at the schools.

Assistance to the family in the preparation and development of the young is how the purpose of school is regarded in Eden.

Also in the audience are numerous college recruiters. Eden is a popular stop for them. Word of academic excellence nowadays gets around almost as quick as a reputation for athletic prowess. Few of the products of Eden's school system will need to take remedial courses before embarking on degree paths. Eden kids do well in college, despite their non-traditional preparation. High school dropouts are rare.

Aside from relatives, the largest number of attendees are teachers. Not just the graduates' mentors from their high school years, but many who had aided in their preparation since pre-kindergarten. In Eden the educational process is seamless: vertically and horizontally **integrated.** This means no content is an isolated body of subject-matter, but is related to other current and future segments of the K-12 curriculum. Math, for example, is taught across many segments, not just as a series of courses for their own sake. History is presented in the light of current events and as part of the "whys" behind other elements in the curriculum. Principles of physics, chemistry, and biology permeate the learning activities whenever applicable.

A *conspiracy* is the closest metaphor I can come up with to describe how Eden views the educational process—a conspiracy joined by the entire community to prepare the young for *accomplished citizenship.* The relationship between the community and the schools is also nearly seamless. The citizens regard, and take literally, that the school is the place where the young are prepared for the kind of society the citizens desire, not just for the limited purpose of teaching isolated academic "subject matter," nor just for the limited purpose of preparing them for their future work-lives.

Graduation is attended by a variety of people from the community as a whole. All are stakeholders in the success of the venture. And, most important, all have contributed to specifying the desired **accomplishments** of the student on completion of K-12. They are all here to celebrate with the youngsters and the teachers their accomplishments thus far. Eden's teachers are the ringleaders in the conspiracy of citizenship preparation.

In Eden the agreed-on purpose for primary and secondary education is to take significant steps in the process of readying the young to be accomplished citizens—citizens of the kind of society Edenites want for the youngsters in the future. The citizenry takes seriously the idea of schools being seamless with society. They are convinced that continued improvement in society must involve the education of the young, but have become disenchanted that the traditional content of the curriculum can achieve such a purpose.

After today, the budding citizens will commence different paths. Some will opt to pursue more specialized preparation in four-year colleges. Others will prepare in community colleges and vocational-technical institutions. Others will join the work force immediately, and receive additional preparation from employers in the particular skills and knowledge required. Some will enter the military. None will be unprepared for whatever they choose. They will be prepared because it was engineered thus. Eden does not tolerate otherwise.

The co-conspirators viewed the proud commencers now receiving their scrolls of accomplishment. They look like an assembly of the United Nations—yellow, brown, white, black. The students also have other individual differences: Different interests, goals, psychomotor ability, genetic makeup, and even intelligence—though Edenites appreciate the many types of intelligence, making it more correct to use the plural. Edenites are also aware of the possible differences in so-called "learning styles," but care about differences only to the degree they might give the teachers clues on selecting the specific instructional tactic appropriate to the student and the content being learned. Eden students are not pigeon-holed or labeled or put in tracks. The educators in Eden know the poor effects of such self-fulfilling expectations. In a sense, there are as many tracks in Eden schools as there are students because the educational process is **individualized** as much as practical.

The families of these young people represent a wide-range of economic circumstances. Many are from single-parent homes. They are fiercely proud that no matter the social, economic, gender, physical, cognitive hand these children of Eden were dealt, the schools and the community guarantee equal *opportunity* to learn, even if they can not guarantee equal *results*. The results of the educational process do, in fact, vary by student. The opportunity does not. Eden engineered it thus. They do not tolerate otherwise.

Eden students from very early in their educational lives are shown the relationship between the content of the curriculum and the possible need in their present and future lives. In fact, the content of the curriculum was *derived* from specification of post-education life expectations. Their classroom is sometimes in the workplaces in the community. Students get a precisely designed opportunity to look first-hand at what it might be like to work in the lab of the local hospital, or be a lawyer or bailiff in the county's courtrooms, or to operate the computer-controlled machinery in the town's manufacturing plants. The teachers are fully aware a major part of the students' lives will be work, thus it is incumbent on the schools to provide facilitating knowledge and skills for that part of the students' future. *Career Preparation* is one of the principle sequences in the K-12 curriculum in Eden, no matter whether a student opts for college, technical school, military, or to enter the work force immediately.

After frequent visits to a wide variety of workplaces, the teachers immediately illustrate the particular knowledge and skill subsets applicable to the work the students had observed. Eden's teachers are always alert to the power of meaningfulness of content to the learning process, and to initiate and maintain the motivation of the learner. The teachers turn almost everything into an opportunity for learning. They are fanatic about it.

Meaningfulness and *worth* of content are guiding principles for whatever is being taught. Geometry is not just a self-contained subject taught in the abstract. It is taught integrated with other "real world" activities, such as when the older students built and sold a modest house under the auspices of the school and under the direction of local craft persons. The purpose of this ambitious venture was not just to teach nail-driving, plumbing, and measuring, but applied practice in geometry, how to deal with financial institutions, planning, scheduling, teamwork, practical physics, problem-solving, work safety, and other knowledge and skills that would be valuable for the rest of their lives. Eden's schools don't aim to produce carpenters or bricklayers. They aim to produce good planners and problem solvers and users of geometry when it is called for. But the carpentry and other overt skills would also come in handy, no matter if the students later opted for work in the building trades or not. A few will.

Eden's schools aim to produce budding citizens with the knowledge and skills relevant to their various *post* K-12 lives, including, but not limited to, further formal education. The meaningfulness and application and value of the content is the center of Eden's educational system. It is the BASE from where they start. WHAT is taught in Eden is derived in a very different way than the traditional approach of starting with macro-categories of subject-matter such as history, science, literature, etc. then presenting the associated knowledge in isolation.

The students are certainly taught concepts and procedures of science, math, history, geography, grammar, and so forth. They do read and interpret good literature. But these subjects are always in context with a goal larger than acquisition of knowledge for its own sake. Adult Edenites are chagrined they previously accepted the categorization of knowledge and skills into artificial subject-matter categories heretofore. They did have some difficulty converting from thinking of knowledge and skills in math, science, history in subject-matter categories. Eden's teachers had even more difficulty changing their paradigm. But they did.

The Eden Conspiracy

The curriculum is not "dumbed down." It is definitely not anti-intellectual. Literacy is one of the more prized outcomes. A rich vocabulary is deemed absolutely necessary. Students read the Great Books just for the enjoyment of it as well as for the lessons illustrated. Life-long learning is actively promoted. Eden's students score high on traditional measures of academic achievement such as standardized tests, but the citizens of Eden don't give as much weight to these as previous. Edenites have come to see such usually measure the learning of subject matter. Edenites are more interested in what the students can *do* and *accomplish* as a result of the instruction, not just the rote regurgitation of isolated facts, or the ability to select the correct answer on a multiple choice exam. Edenites are more interested in referencing student accomplishments against performance criteria, rather than the norms for age groups. Though it is obvious students must learn facts and basic knowledge and skills to do so, the real aim of education in Eden is the acquisition of behavioral processes they'll need to be successful as citizens—including the prerequisites for further formal education and life-long learning.

To illustrate, the children of Eden are often assigned as homework to play the *Mom, Let Me Show You How to…* game. Examples:

Let me show you how to

… *spot faulty reasoning in a newspaper advertisement.*
… *construct and test hypotheses like a scientist does.*
… *interpret nutrition labels on food.*
… *write a letter of complaint.*
… *interpret information presented in a matrix.*
… *translate commonly used foreign phrases.*
… *tell difference between a claim and a fact.*
… *calculate cost of a loan at several interest rates.*
… *convert a passive voice sentence to active.*
… *defuse anger in a hostile person.*
… *make oral presentations using deduction and induction.*
… *spot faulty grammar of a sportscaster.*
… *calculate percent of calories from fat in a meal.*

... weigh pros and cons of purchase options.
... prepare for a job interview.
... budget time for a month's schedule.
... summarize a long article into main points.
... calculate the square feet of our house.
... tell the difference between a "want" and a "need."

The teachers as conspiracy ringleaders not only take literally the overall educational aim of accomplished citizen-preparation, but are masters of engineering HOW the content is taught. They were all trained in procedures for analysis and design of instructional events to make it highly likely the students will learn relevant and valuable knowledge and skills. Eden teachers did not learn in the colleges of education the precision approach to teaching they now practice. Teachers who somehow managed to become accomplished teachers seem to have learned effective teaching methods by trial and error.

Not in Eden. In the redesign of the educational system, not only did Eden take a very different approach to deriving what was to be taught, but invested in retraining teachers to be successful in HOW the knowledge and skills should be taught. To do this Eden sought the help of the few private and public institutions who were practicing methods for an **accomplishment-based, precision approach to instruction.** They funded this considerable effort via grants, contributions from non-profit professional organizations, and sharing of teacher training materials from interested businesses and industries in their state. (Some American businesses and industries adopted sophisticated instructional methodologies long before public education.)

The teachers were astonished at the existence of methods and techniques of instruction they had never heard of: an *Instructional Science*—instructional design and delivery techniques that are precise, and result in high levels of learning even for those who were previously considered to be "educationally disadvantaged" and incapable of exemplary accomplishment.

Eden teachers learned techniques for designing instruction, study, and practice activities to increase the retention of knowledge and skills; how to produce *fluent* learning; and, how to give various types of feedback.

Eden teachers were taught how to operate a system for individualizing instruction to take care of varying learning rates of students, the differing ability levels, the differing goals of students, and how to accommodate differing learning styles as much as practical.

The teachers became experts at evaluating and selecting computer-assisted and paper-based instructional programs available to them from the growing number of publishers of instructional software. The teachers found this a little frustrating because the state-of-the-art of this field is still somewhat primitive. Many wound up developing some of their own materials. This evolved into sort of a cottage industry for selling these to other school systems.

The conspiracy ringleaders in Eden are not "gifted" teachers, if one means by that oft-heard phrase that they do something mysterious, unexplainable, and either-you-have-it-or-you-don't. Eden's teachers are accomplished at their profession because they themselves have accepted the concepts and practice of deriving content from a non-traditional base—the specification of knowledge and skills of an accomplished citizen. Eden's teachers are accomplished at their profession because they themselves became students of, and practiced in Instructional Science. The teachers were given the opportunity to become accomplished at their profession, *as measured by the performance of their students*, because they had the full support of the educational administration in the city and from the community at-large.

Eden's teachers are masters at dealing with student motivation, not from fuzzy and suspect aims such as "building self-esteem," but because they have become fluent in using techniques involving when and how to give feedback, when and how arrange positive consequences for the student. But by and large, their students are motivated because of the *meaningfulness* of the content, and because their success is carefully engineered by the conspirators. (Edenites have come to realize confidence is a by-product of competence, not the other way around.) The students' motivation is also affected because they are not in an environment of threat and coercion. (Edenites have come to realize that threat and coercion tend to be DE-motivating.) The students are also motivated because of high expectations, not only from their teachers, but from the community as a whole. It is a conspiracy after all.

Graduation Day has come to an end in Eden. The smiling, and occasionally tearful, young citizens join their relatives and friends. The citizens have confidence in them because they have contributed to their accomplishments. The kids will now leave their designed and engineered educational environment to live in comparatively undesigned and chaotic worlds. It cannot be guaranteed they will become truly successful and accomplished citizens. The only guarantee is they will have the prerequisites for it and have a fighting chance. Eden has engineered it thus. They do not tolerate otherwise.

Though Medianville and Eden are fantasies, the data from one of the cities are real. Unfortunately, that city is Medianville. The parade of deficits and data listed (dropout rate, low literacy, high teen pregnancy, poor math performance etc.) represent the actual findings of numerous studies performed on our nation's educational system. And, the list of interventions taken in the synthesized city of Medianville (raise teacher's salaries, smaller classes, back-to-basics, computers and so forth) are also the more frequent interventions recommended and implemented in effort to improve education in America. By and large, they have not worked. And, more of the same, as currently proposed, will not either.

Medianville is close to reality. Eden is only a product of my visioning. Though some approximation of some of the interventions Eden took might have been tried previously, nowhere to my knowledge has such a massive re-design of education taken place—especially the seemingly radical revision of the BASE from which the content of the curriculum is derived—what I call an *accomplishment-base*. Thus, the previous description of Eden's approach to educational reform did not list measured results. That can only be speculated for now. But I believe the results would be astonishing---not only high levels of learning for a large majority of students, but the acquisition knowledge and skills that would transfer to the students' post-school lives.

The problems with education are worse than even the most concerned believe. It is not only that the traditional measures of education (achievement-test scores, SAT scores, dropout rates and so forth) are falling or staying flat, the content (what we teach) does not transfer to post-education life in a very large majority of the students. Thus, the inescapable conclusion is that not only are we not teaching well, but we are wasting valuable human and economic resources by the traditional subject-matter-based approach to deriving content. Thus, the first major thesis of this book is:

> **No matter which one, or which combination of the educational reform measures is adopted, it will have only a marginal effect, at best, to improve the post-school performance of the majority of our young people. We must derive WHAT is to be taught in a fundamentally different way.**

If it is not worth teaching at all. It is not worth teaching well.

Why and how we might produce actual Edens by this approach is the subject of this book. As a preview, it might be useful to compare and contrast the two educational reform approaches followed in Medianville and Eden…

Element:	Medianville:	Eden:
Aim of the effort:	To improve education	To improve education
Purpose of Education:	Provide opportunity for the young to acquire knowledge of traditional subject matter	Produce graduates who have skills, knowledge and attitudes to become accomplished citizens
Relationship to community as a whole:	School is a self-contained entity	School is seamless with the community (A "conspiracy")
Methodology used:	Brainstorming of interventions	Problem-solving process to determine interventions
Base for the content in the curriculum:	Traditional subject-matter catedories	Desired accomplishments post-school
Input to decision concerning content:	Educators only	All stakeholders in the community
Overall curriculum design:	Courses are self-contained entities	Courses are seamless and integrated
Learning activities:	Traditional teach-then-test knowledge	Precisely designed teaching tactics drawn from Instructional Science
Methods for impacting teachers:	Emphasis on teacher motivation	Training of teachers to become Instructional Science Practitioners

Purpose and Goals in Educational Eden

We simply don't have a good idea of the purposes of education. It is largely an aimless affair.

–Thomas F. Gilbert
Human Competence

Eden undertook a radical redesign of formal education. Unlike Medianville, it followed a systematic problem-solving process to do so by addressing these issues in this exact order:

1. *What is the ultimate PURPOSE of education? What are the general GOALS of education suggested by the purpose?*
2. *What are the student ACCOMPLISHMENTS desired as a result of the educational process?*
3. *What is the GAP between current accomplishments and desired accomplishments? What are the root-CAUSES of the gap? What SOLUTIONS (interventions) are therefore indicated?*
4. *What CONTENT should be taught?*
5. *How should education be REDESIGNED and DELIVERED? How should it be EVALUATED?*

Medianville either ignored or made assumptions about issues 1-4 and brainstormed the redesign. Eden redesigned and delivered instruction based on findings of 1-4.

If we seek to redesign anything, it implies there is evidence the present entity is no longer meeting its PURPOSE to the degree desired. We might redesign a building to remediate problems with existing work functions, such as moving walls to decrease inefficiency of work. Engineers "go back to the drawing board" (redesign) when a system does not meet the intended purpose. Physicians redesign, so to speak, when they perceive the general purpose (*proper functioning of the body*) is not being achieved. They then engage in a diagnostic process: Specify how the present condition of the patient deviates from the desired state, and then find the cause(s) of the gap. Physicians then prescribe treatment ("interventions"), based on the probable causes of the deficiency. Accomplished physicians do not brainstorm interventions. Nor does the accomplished physician have a universally applied treatment no matter the cause of the problem.

I think a majority of Americans believe education needs reformation (redesign). But even the more vocal of educational reformers lack much agreement on the interventions needed. I believe a contributing reason for this non-agreement is that the five issues aforementioned have not been addressed systematically and in the order listed. The difficulty begins when we skip the first issue: *What is the ultimate purpose of education?*

Purpose of
EDUCATION

Statement and agreement on purpose is key to the design of anything new. Re-examination of purpose is key to redesign of existing entities. It is remarkable the number of human enterprises that engage in furious activity with no pre-specified purpose, much less follow a problem-solving progression to generate relevant interventions. An even greater number of programs are undertaken where the participants in the activities have purpose and goals that are different from their fellows without making this known and arbitrating a common purpose. Regard the differing-purposes issue in the Vietnam debacle. Working-at-cross-purposes is a common cause of problems of committees and teams. Businesses without clear purpose soon cease to exist.

The last 10 years have seen rather massive efforts to reform education. Many books and commissions have offered a wide variety of redesign suggestions—some comparatively mild, some radical. There have been scores of pilot programs and blue-ribbon panels. Only some of these have begun at the beginning: Agreeing on the desired ultimate outcome of education is the purpose.

When talking to groups about education, I always begin with the question: *What is the general purpose of education?* The question, no matter to whom it is addressed, seems to surprise them. Most seem to think the answer is obvious to everyone. Probing, I find a wide variety of statements of purpose. The persons who give most pause and seem to have most difficulty with the question are educators. For example, when asked as an open-ended question to primary school teachers, I've heard:

- *To prepare them for middle school*
- *To teach them the basics*
- *To build their self-esteem*
- *To teach them to enjoy learning*

When asked of high school teachers:

- *To prepare them for further education*
- *To get them to appreciate my subject-matter*
- *To help them to develop their individual potential*

When asked of college of education faculties, I seem to get very philosophical statements such as:

- *To promote learning for learning's sake*
- *To foster understanding of the human condition*
- *To nurture the range of ethical, physical, spiritual, intellectual, and aesthetic qualities of mankind*

Parents often respond about how education should give their children information so the child *will have it better than I had it.* When asked what the *it* in the sentence means, they usually talk about earning a good living and coping with everyday problems of life.

Predictably, employers respond with purposes having to do with preparing the young for their future working life.

The agreement on general purpose of education is important because the way we define purpose will greatly influence the specific goals of the enterprise. And, the nature of the goals we seek will, in time, shape the activities and interventions implemented to achieve those goals. If purpose is unstated, then specific goals will tend to be missing or arbitrary. One might say education without a stated purpose is *purposeless*.

In the past, the apparent purpose of education seems to have reflected the characteristic of society. In the early years of our country schools were modeled on a European design—attended by sons of the elite; who were taught Latin, Greek, and a curriculum of the classics. The idea of education-for-all came much later. In the middle years of America, when the country had a mostly rural population, most of the schools seemed to reflect the purposes of an agrarian society—enough of the 3 R's to facilitate farming and marketing of crops, usually terminating when the kids were old enough to be productive field hands. For the most part, only those who aspired to the ministry, law, medicine or the military received further schooling.

The combination of the waves of immigrants to wash on America's shore and the Industrial Revolution precipitated the factory model of education: large numbers of students in progressive grades being taught, in a lock-step manner, enough subject-matter to integrate them into our culture, and to enable them to do the manual labor jobs of the time.

I don't think schools now reflect the needs of the present-day society, much less the coming society many portend will be radically different.

There is a wistfulness of some who want education to "return to what schools used to be." It is common to think of the "good old days" in education as well as nostalgia for life in general. Note this comment from Arthur Bestor in *Educational Wastelands:*

> *There is a general dissatisfaction with the results of 12 years of education currently provided by most of our public schools. Businessmen are dismayed at the deficiencies in reading, writing, and arithmetic displayed by the high school and college graduates they employ. Parents are alarmed at the educational handicaps under which their children are obliged to labor as they enter the serious business of life.*

The above was penned in 1953! Now almost a half-century later, despite the last 15 years of educational reform and billions of dollars spent, the same cry is heard. Schools were almost always a dreary and punishing place for the majority of students; and, more important, they were largely unsuccessful even in achieving the purpose of the time. Drop-outs were higher than today. Measured results were lower. I fear there never were the good old days of education.

It would be overtly presumptuous of me to try and dictate the general purpose of education, but I must admit to strong bias about the importance of starting with clear purposes and goals, and obtaining agreement on them. Having spent all of my professional life assisting educational organizations in industry, business, and government in the design and redesign of programs to affect human performance, I've seen the dramatic effect it can have when we first concentrate on ends before we look at means; that is, define and agree on purpose and goals. This effort is relatively simple and is apt to yield great returns. Education is not the same as business, but they do share the need for agreed-on purposes and goals to be successful.

I've learned it is more useful to state purpose and goals in terms of ENDS (outputs, results, accomplishments) instead of processes or actions. For example, *To make Product X* is not statement of purpose. It is a general statement of a process. The ultimate end (purpose) is *Customer satisfaction from Product X at a profit.* The phrase *to teach reading* describes process. The desired end (purpose) is *literacy.* I submit the overall desired outcome of the educational process is NOT merely *to teach principles, concepts, and facts* of given subject-matters.

What, then, should be the overall purpose of education? Again, I must admit to considerable bias about the matter. My bias could have its roots in an epiphany of sort that took place the first day of the fourth grade many decades ago.

I, and my fellow nine year-olds, had started three years earlier as an eager bunch, primed with anticipation of school and all the swell things we'd learn. The intervening three years had squelched a good deal of the motivation for many of us. We had resigned to the fact that school was mostly boredom, bad lunches, and big people threatening us. In that time some of us learned to read a little about the exploits of kids named Dick and Jane. We could do some ciphers. We spent a lot of time filling in black and white drawings with crayons. We never questioned, of course, the ultimate purpose of all this. Everybody said it was a good idea. We went along. What do kids at that age know about what is good for them?

On the first day of the fourth grade a new teacher, Miz Morris, surveyed the silent room. I thought she looked a little like my Aunt Lilly. Her eyes stopped on me for some reason.

Joseph, why do we go to school?

To learn stuff, I said with remarkable insight.

Yes, that's certainly true. Learning is what school is about. Peggy, why do you think we go to school? (Miz Morris would prove to be a master of induction.)

To learn reading, arithmetic, spelling and all. (I don't recall resenting her for the better answer. I had a crush on Peggy.)

True. We do come to school to learn those things. But do you think there might be a bigger reason?

Yeah, called out Bubba from the back of the room. *My daddy'd whup me if I didn't!* (Giggles from the 30 of us. Bubba was the class clown.)

Well, I don't know about that, Miz Morris said, restraining a smile. *But I want y'all to always remember the real reason you go to school is to learn things that will help you become a high-quality person in life.*

Now, I didn't have a much of a formed idea about what *high quality* meant, but I really liked the sound of it then. I still do. Maybe it is the root-cause of this book.

Since that dawn age in time, I've sat in hundreds of classrooms. I don't know if I'd now equate to Miz Morris' idea of what a *quality person* is because she never defined it. Nor did the hundreds of subsequent teachers, college instructors, and graduate school professors I've had. But I believe that Miz Morris was correct in her stated intent about the overall end of education. I now suggest the overall purpose of formal education should be:

To produce graduates who have skills, knowledge, information, and attitudes to become ACCOM-PLISHED CITIZENS.

If one would substitute Miz Morris' *quality* with *accomplished*, the intent would be almost the same. (Why I use the term *accomplished* will become apparent in a subsequent chapter.)

A *citizen* is a person owing allegiance to and entitled to the protection of a given society; and, one who is entitled to certain rights and privileges.

Accomplished in this context is intended to connote that the citizen has acquired and practices certain abilities valued by society.

These questions immediately come to mind: What are these abilities? Who should specify these abilities? What needs to be learned to facilitate these abilities? How should this be taught?

The bulk of this book explores those questions, and are embodied in the five major issues listed at the start of this chapter.

One might say the aforementioned purpose I have burdened education with is among the purposes of society as a whole. I agree. I think one of the purposes of society is the protection and preparation of the young. Like the citizens of Eden, I believe that schools and society as a whole should be almost seamless and conspiratorial. A few educational reformers seem to agree with the citizens of Eden...

- *Most people can learn everything they need to know to be good citizens and successful participants in the American economy.* (President Clinton's remarks to Governor's Educational Summit, March, 1996.)
- *Systems of learning and human development should co-evolve with the larger society as well as spearhead societal evolution.* (Bela H. Banathy, *Systems Design of Education*)
- *...public education should prepare young people for a role as citizens of a democracy.* (Louis V. Gerstner, *Reinventing Education*)
- (Education should) *equip American young people to function as workers, citizens, and civilized human beings.* (Edward B. Fiske, *Smart Schools, Smart Kids*)
- *A back-to-basics movement is a good idea, but only if it is oriented to competency in life, citizenship, and work.* (Daniel W. Rossides, "The Worthless Debate Continues" in *The Great School Debate*)

My offered purpose, *...to become accomplished citizens,* implies that schools and society should be seamless. That is, education is a sub-set of society and should therefore reflect the values of society. Speaking only for myself, I want a society with at least these characteristics:

- Exists under a democratic form of government.
- Is lawful, orderly, ethical, and safe.
- Allows freedom for its citizens—within the law.
- Allows freedom for enterprise—within the law.
- Provides equal opportunity for its citizens.

- Values the family as the basic unit of society.
- In partnership with the family, provides protection and development of the young.

The desired characteristics of society not only bias us toward engineering the kind of community we want, but have implications for the content of education and the design of the educational process. If we don't proactively design the kind of society we want, then it will happen chaotically. If we don't design the kind of education we want, it will continue to be chaotic.

For example, stakeholders might require schools to have objectives to teach content relating to law, orderliness, ethics, safety, democracy, and so forth. Though it will be a matter of some controversy when precise description of these generalities occurs, the link between desired societal values and the purpose and goals of education is the important point. As Roger Kaufman put it in *Mapping Educational Success:*

> *Strategic thinking for education depends on developing an ideal vision of tomorrow and identifying the contributions of our schools, curriculum, and methods to reach the preferred future. Without an ideal vision, we limit thinking and planning to re-active, here-and-now, quick-fix tactics.*

Goals of
EDUCATION

Without an agreed-on purpose, a statement of goals is apt to be arbitrary. Purpose points the way to more specific goals. In fact, goals are merely more specific statements of purpose. For example, a physician's general purpose is to produce a *properly functioning body of the patient*. That is the overall desired output. This purpose can then be described in terms of more specific goals:

- *Properly functioning nervous system*
- *Properly functioning circulatory system*
- *Properly functioning digestive system* and so forth.

If one accepts the overall purpose of education is *to produce accomplished citizens*, what then might be the goals? In order to specify these, we need to have a scheme that represents the components or subsets that collectively define the purpose. I find it useful to describe these subsets in terms of the various roles the student will play in life. Thus, we might describe educational goals as *to give students skills/knowledge/information/attitudes to become accomplished:*

- *Society members*
- *Family members*
- *Workers*
- *Individuals*

Those goals indicate a very different paradigm from the traditional goals of formal education which seem to be: *to teach math; to teach history; to teach science* and the like. A goal guides us in a direction. A goal is the BASE from which we operate. One should note the traditional goals of education indicate a subject-matter base. Such a base directs education toward ends which have to do with acquirement of knowledge, skills, information *within* subject-matter categories, and therein lies the problem.

The goals I propose above indicate a different base: post-school LIFE. These goals would lead education in a very much different direction. The goals provide a superstructure for addressing more specific educational goals in terms of desired student *accomplishments.*

An *accomplishment* is an OUTPUT produced that is relevant and valuable to a goal. For example, if I have the goal of achieving *a harmonious family life,* then perhaps some of the accomplishments I must produce to achieve that end might include:

- *A plan for family interactions*
- *Communication with spouse*
- *Communication with children*
- *Resolutions of conflicts*

Desired student accomplishments become the foundation ("base") for educational reform, especially in the matter of deciding what to teach.

4. What is an Accomplishment Base?

The first basic premise of this book is that education should be purposeful, goal-driven and accomplishment-based

(This is in contrast to the traditional subject-matter base where knowledge is grouped in the familiar categories we have used for generations.) The specification of the desired student accomplishments as a result of the educational process is especially pivotal in deriving WHAT should be taught.

I use the term *accomplishment* instead of *output* or *outcome* or *result* because accomplishment suggests quality, worthiness, and value. (The term, in this context, came into popular use in Thomas Gilbert's landmark book *Human Competence*.)

When we describe someone's accomplishment, we almost always focus on an OUTPUT:

- *Madame Curie won the <u>Nobel Prize</u>.*
- *Alexander Graham Bell invented the <u>telephone</u>.*
- *Bear Bryant won six <u>National Championships</u>.*
- *Mary produced the highest number of <u>sales</u>.*
- *John produced a high-quality <u>poem</u>.*

Note in each case above, the output is a noun. The focus of each description is on a result, NOT a process. The phrase does not give direct honor to the knowledge (input) of the accomplisher.

Purposes and goals are useful to state the overall intent and direction of education, even when stated in the very broad terms shown in the previous chapter. Also, when the purpose and goals are stated in terms of general accomplishment, more specific targets are made more likely to be in accomplishment terms. For example, given one of the broad educational goals: *To produce graduates who have skills/knowledge/information to become accomplished SOCIETY MEMBERS*, major student accomplishments could then be specified subordinate to that goal. Examples of major accomplishments under that goal:

- *Obedience to the law*
- *Informed voting decisions*
- *Contributions to stable environment*

- *Resolution of interpersonal conflict*
- *Contributions to community improvement*

An accomplishment is a valuable output of a PROCESS or actions or behaviors. A human accomplishment is the end result of a person DOING/THINKING something. For example, one of a physician's desired accomplishments is *a specification of the cause of a health problem.* The accomplishment is produced by the physician engaging in the process of *diagnosis.* Further, the diagnostic process is conducted given INPUTS such as *patient symptoms.*

Knowledge, skills, information, and student attitudes are inputs in education. Given these, we want the student to be able to perform processes such as problem solving, finding information, and making decisions so that they produce accomplishments of value to the goals.

As discussed later, the content of the curriculum is derived by starting with specification of the desired accomplishments, not by starting with the inputs.

Schematically, we represent the relationship of the three terms :

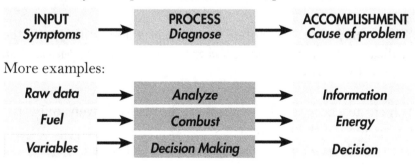

| INPUT | PROCESS | ACCOMPLISHMENT |
| Symptoms | Diagnose | Cause of problem |

More examples:

Raw data	Analyze	Information
Fuel	Combust	Energy
Variables	Decision Making	Decision

Inputs by themselves are not important unless they are processed. What good are raw data (inputs) unless they are analyzed (process)? By the same token, it is not the processes that are of ultimate importance. It is the RESULT of the process that we value—the accomplishment.

For example, suppose our *goal* is *improved living condition*. We hire a builder to engage in the building process. The builder determines what *inputs* (lumber, bricks etc.) are needed. At the bottom line, we judge the builder by quality of the house that is produced (*accomplishment*).

Processes are not good in themselves. We don't give A's for effort. We give them for accomplishment. Also, we don't directly value knowledge inputs. For example, which person below would you tend to hire for a sales position, given only the information in these statements?

   Candidate A says: *I've completed 10 courses on selling.*
   Candidate B says: *I work hard. I make more calls than anyone.*
   Candidate C says: *I produced the highest sales in my district.*

Which paramedic do you want to attend to your child who has stopped breathing, given only the information in these statements?

   A: *I know how a resuscitator works.*
   B: *I can work a resuscitator.*
   C: *I have produced many resuscitations.*

(I'm reminded of the not-so-funny expression common in the medical profession: *The operation was successful, but the patient died.* Success lies in results.)

Which teacher should we value the most, given only the information in these statements?

   A: *I know a large amount of facts about the subject.*
   B: *I work very hard at teaching.*
   C: *My students have important knowledge and skills as a result of my instruction.*

In each of the three examples above, "A" is remarking on input (knowledge); "B" is commenting on behavioral processes; "C" describes an ACCOMPLISHMENT.

It is the *outputs* of the educational process we should judge to be valuable or not valuable—the student accomplishments.

A process always produces an output, valuable or not. In education, we should be interested in *valuable* outputs. Thus, I use the term *accomplishment* to connote: *a valuable output the student produces.* As goals are more specific statements of purpose, accomplishments are more specific statements of goals.

It seems to me we should first determine the desired accomplishments before attending to the inputs (knowledge) or processes (teaching) of education. And, as stated, we should attend to the purpose and goals of education before attending to the desired outputs.

Using the Input-Process-Accomplishment paradigm, we want this desired progression to occur:

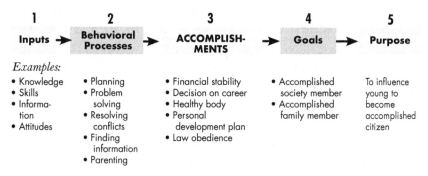

Education occurs in 1-2-3-4-5 order, but we should redesign education in 5-4-3-2-1 order. That is, we first address purpose, then goals, then accomplishments, then processes, then inputs. It is critical to do any design work in this reverse-order sequence, especially educational design.

Making the paradigm-shift to think in accomplishment terms seems to be difficult for many people. I have to prompt myself frequently with these mnemonics: *Behavior, I do at the time; accomplishments, I leave behind.* And, *processes are what we see while they are working; outputs are what we see when they stop working.*

Incidentally, one should not misconstrue that I'm saying the ends-justify-the-means. I'm merely saying the ends might help us *derive* the means and increase the chances the means are relevant and valuable.

In business, inputs and processes are COSTS, but we obtain RETURN from accomplishments. I need knowledgeable workers (inputs) in order to perform high quality work (processes) in order to make a quality product (output). Investors buy a company's stock based on its past and potential accomplishments such as earnings, profits, market share etc. They do not buy the stock of companies who have the most number of Ph.D.'s working for them.

In past educational reform efforts there has been much emphasis on inputs, but not much attention to the desired behavioral processes we want the students to be able to do, and even less attention paid to desired ends. As stated, purposes and goals are usually assumed. Outputs are usually thought of in terms of grades, exam scores, and number of courses taken.

If we can agree on the general goals of education as being primarily to produce graduates who are in the process of becoming accomplished society members, family members, workers, and individuals, then we can address the issue: What should be the general student accomplishments within each role indicated in the goals?

Who should specify the
ACCOMPLISHMENTS?

It would be presumptuous of me to specify these accomplishments and try to dictate them to education. (A later chapter lists examples of accomplishments stakeholders told me they wanted.) I suggest it would be presumptuous for any individual or single-issue group to do so. Yet, this is similar to what we do when we leave the decision of *what*-to-teach to the state and to teachers. The specification of purpose, goals, and desired accomplishments are matters for the STAKEHOLDERS in education. The stakeholders include almost everyone in society: parents, employers, educators, and citizens at large—a conspiracy for the development of the young. Chester Finn, in *We Must Take Charge*, agrees:

> . . . . *the public that needs to take charge [of education] includes bus drivers and dental hygienists, truck gardeners, and viola players. In certain domains, such as the requisites of economic competitiveness, we may be especially receptive to the advice of business tycoons. But when considering curricular content, school organization, and countless other matters, the hog butcher in Sioux City has as much standing as the CEO in Manhattan.*

My proposal that we start with a different base for education and work backward could lead to revolutionary changes in both the content of curricula and how the knowledge and skills and information relevant to desired accomplishments are taught. I have not underestimated the difficulty of the radical change that will be required in the way almost all of us view education. For what I'm proposing would undoubtedly lead to a fundamental change in *what* we teach and *how* we teach it. **I propose abandoning a subject-matter base for education in favor of a different base: The accomplishments desired by the stakeholders.**

Following the work-backward-from-purpose approach (which is, incidentally, the fundamental method for the design of any system) would lead ultimately to the specification of the specific information/knowledge/skills, and perhaps attitudes and values, we teach in school. This is because the accomplishments desired would suggest the behavioral processes needing to be learned; and, the behavioral processes would suggest the specific content needed as inputs.

For example, given a desired major accomplishment such as *economic stability*, then the acquisition of these general behavioral processes might be suggested: *budgeting, financing, purchasing, saving, investing.* Then, the knowledge/skills/information/ attitudes underpinning each of the above might need to be taught. For example, the behavioral process *purchasing* might require learning how to:

- *Discriminate needs from wants*
- *Compare cost/benefits of alternatives*
- *Determine if can be afforded*
- *Read a warranty*

We could then easily analyze each of those increments of knowledge/skill to determine the specific "basics" needed to facilitate the behaviors; for example, the relevant principles, relevant math operations, relevant vocabulary and so forth. How this can be done will be explored later in this book.

Previously, I suggested that a problem-solving procedure be followed when attempting educational reform. The next chapter outlines my approach for such a diagnostic and prescriptive procedure.

The Eden Conspiracy

5. Problems, Causes, Solutions in Education

Miseducation is not a function of a child's race or neighborhood, but of teaching methods he or she is exposed to from kindergarten on.

—Marva Collins
Marva Collins' Way

A frequent recommendation of educational reformers is that students need to be taught "problem solving." However they usually don't define what such means in any helpful detail. I rarely see any evidence they practice what they preach. As stated earlier, specification of interventions should be the output of a problem solving process, not the start. A problem solving progression is appropriate for the front-end of efforts to redesign education because the aim of problem solving is to yield the appropriate interventions (solutions).

If we reduce most formal problem solving methods to their essence, it boils down to a three-part sequence:
1. **Define the problem**
2. **Determine the cause**
3. **Determine the solution**

Most problem solving methodologists agree the effort must progress in the 1-2-3 sequence above and no other. One should not start out with a given solution and look for a problem to apply it to—though having a solution-in-search-of-a-problem is common in education.

PROBLEMS

People use the term *problem* loosely, but mainstream problem solving methodologists often define it as a deficit or a "gap"— the difference between what *is* and what-*should*-be. This assumes one has defined and agreed on the problem-free or desirable situation—the should-be. For example, a general statement of a problem according to that definition: *Harless is not healthy.* This implies the problem-stator knows what the desirable state of health is and what mine is.

Coupling this with the previous discussion, another way of defining a problem at the most general level is: The intended PURPOSE of something is not being met. If one accepts the general purpose of education is *to produce graduates who have skills/ knowledge/information/attitudes to become accomplished citizens*, then we must consider if current education is, in fact, satisfactorily filling this purpose. If we decide it is not, then we would define the problem at its most general level as simply: **Education is not producing graduates who have appropriate skills/knowledge/ information/ attitudes to become accomplished citizens.**

If one does not agree with my previously offered purpose of education, then this general problem statement would also not be accepted. Many will not agree with my statement of the general problem because they view education as having a much narrower purpose. One might also suggest that a general problem is *parents are not preparing their children satisfactorily in the process of becoming accomplished citizens.* If so, I'd tend to agree; but the issue being discussed at the moment is the need for educational reform. (Child-rearing reform will be the subject of future presumptions.)

As the purpose points the way to more specific goals, then problems can be defined more specifically as deficits in meeting goals. For example, if I have a personal purpose to be *healthy*, I then must have the relevant goals: *properly functioning nervous system; properly functioning circulatory system; properly functioning gastrointestinal system* etc.

If so, then more specific statements of *problems* would be:
- *Harless' nervous system is not functioning properly.*
- *Harless' circulatory system is not functioning properly.*

In other words, there are deficiencies in achieving goals, thus more finite statements of problems.

If one accepts the goals of education are: *To produce graduates who have S/K/I/A to become accomplished members of society; accomplished workers; accomplished family members; and accomplished in their individual life,* then we might specify these more finite possible problems:

- *Education is not producing students satisfactorily to become accomplished in their life as an INDIVIDUAL.*
- *Education is not preparing students satisfactorily to become accomplished FAMILY MEMBERS.*
- *Education is not preparing students satisfactorily to become accomplished WORKERS.*
- *Education is not preparing students satisfactorily to become accomplished SOCIETY members.*

It is possible to further analyze each of the above into more specific statements in terms of deficit accomplishments. For example, *Education is not preparing students satisfactorily to: make informed voting decisions; to resolve conflicts,* etc. But for the big-picture purpose of this book, I will stop at the goal-level statement of problems.

In order to say any one or all of the above is a problem, we must have evidence it so and the degree it is so. For example, considering the problem statement: *Education is not preparing students satisfactorily to become accomplished workers,* examples of pieces of evidence which might support the general case the problem exists:

- NY Telephone screened 57,000 applicants to find 2,000 with sufficient entry skills and knowledge to enter training to become operators and repair technicians.
- 80% of applicants for entry jobs at Motorola failed to achieve minimum scores on tests.
- 85% of 118 large companies surveyed said schools failed to teach anything about the world of work.
- 25% of the Navy's recruits cannot read at the minimum level sufficient to understand safety instructions.

- American companies spend billions for remedial education for new employees.

For the problem statement: *Education is not preparing students satisfactorily to become accomplished members of society,* examples of possibly relevant evidence:
- Less than 50% of high school students ever performed any kind of public service.
- Juvenile arrest rate has doubled since 1960.
- Nearly 1,000,000 drop out of high school each year. (Rate is as high as 60% in some areas. Over 25% nationwide.) Half will appear before a judge within 5 years.
- More than 10% admit to having brought a weapon to school.
- In 1997 crimes of violence by teens was 10 times that of Canada.
- Homicide is second leading cause of death among teenagers and young adults.
- Nearly half of adults are not above a basic level of literacy.
- A low percentage of young adults vote.

For the problem statement: *Education is not preparing students satisfactorily to become accomplished individuals,* examples of possible evidence:
- 68% of high school seniors did not know income taxes must be paid on savings account interest.
- 30% think Social Security is retirement income received from an employer.
- 51% did not know that income tax rates rise as income rises.
- Credit problems are almost epidemic in young adults.

CAUSES

In problem solving we have a basic rule: *The solution to a problem must match the cause.* In other words, the nature of the cause indicates the solution. If a physician finds an infection (problem) as a result of bacterial growth (cause), then the physician administers an antibiotic (solution). If the physician misdiagnoses the CAUSE, then the wrong intervention is likely to be implemented and the problem is not solved or minimized.

If the cause of some problem is a lack of knowledge/skill/ information, then we prescribe an educational intervention. If the cause of a problem is the lack of desire, we seek a solution that is motivational in nature—a change in consequences or incentives, for example, not an educational type of solution.

Those of us who are practitioners of a problem solving process realize any given problem can, and usually does, have a combination of causes. If so, then a combination of solutions (interventions) is warranted. This is one of the reasons why single-intervention education reform efforts have not worked as well as hoped. This is in addition to massive misdiagnosis of the fundamental causes of problems in education.

For example, suppose an organization had this problem: *Salespersons are not producing sufficient sales of Product X.* The solution warranted is not known until the cause(s) is determined. If a contributing cause is found to be a *lack of skills/knowledge concerning sales techniques*, then the indicated single-intervention would be education in sales techniques. Suppose an additional contributing cause was found to be *price of Product X is much higher than the competition*, then an additional solution must also be found, such as making the price more competitive. A common error is to treat one of the causes and hope the problem will be solved. It rarely is. A combination of causes requires a combination of solutions.

The purpose of any intervention is to eliminate the root-causes of problems or at least to minimize their effects. For instance, suppose an organization had this problem: *Salespersons are not producing sufficient sales of Product X.* Suppose this cause was found to account for the problem: *They are not provided good prospects by the marketing organization.* Eliminating the root-cause would involve getting the marketing organization to provide better leads. An example of minimizing-the-effects would be to teach the salespersons how to generate their own leads.

There is no single cause of the problems in education. Therefore, there must be a combination of solutions. In addition, the root-causes of the problems cannot always be eliminated. Therefore, some interventions will need to be prescribed to minimize the effects. For instance, the much publicized Head Start program is a macro application of such reasoning. Head Start seeks to minimize the effect of the root-cause of children not entering the K-12 sequence with the expected prerequisites others have acquired from home. (This is not to say whether Head Start works or not, but merely an example of an intervention which seeks to minimize negative effects.)

Looking at each macro-statement of education problems, we could speculate a long list of possible causes. I believe **one of the fundamental causes is most educators don't view that the purpose of education is to prepare students to become accomplished citizens.** In other words, there is a fundamental disagreement on general purpose and therefore goals. Educators almost invariably operate from a different base than desired post-school accomplishment. They operate from a subject-matter base, which implies a purpose different from the premise of this book.

As stated, I always begin discussion of educational improvement with every group by asking the question: *What is the prime purpose of education?* The most frequent reaction from educators is silence. When they do respond, comments about a purpose having to do with facilitating the student's future lives are quite rare. Parents, however, usually talk about purpose having to do with preparation for life. So do employers.

As part of the research for this book, I asked 160 teachers: *How do you decide the CONTENT in your subject?* The results:

- Content required for students' next level
  of academics 48%
- Content experts in my subject say is
  important 36%
- Content applicable to students'
  lives after schooling 10%
- Content students express interest
  in learning 6%
- Content the community wants students
  to learn 0%

I also asked the teachers: *How often have you consulted parents or employers in the community as an input to deciding content?* The results:

- Very frequently 0%
- Often 0%
- A few times 12%
- Never 88%

This small sample seems to support my distinct impression that most educators see education and society as somewhat distinct entities, not seamless as it is in Eden. Many teachers and school boards seem to assume the purpose of school is to teach facts, concepts, and principles under the somewhat arbitrary domains called "subjects."

It is not surprising that teachers believe education should be subject-matter based. A subject-matter base for content of education is what educators have seen their entire lives. They have not been shown an alternative. Even in primary grades their teachers moved from one subject to the next during the day. In middle and high school their teachers were specialists in a subject-matter. In college the neophyte teachers themselves usually sought to become specialists in a subject-matter. We tend to teach WHAT we've been taught.

Teaching knowledge under the general subject-matter categories is what teachers are hired to do because schooling is now organized from a subject-matter base. The state often dictates the content, and it is invariably subject-matter-based.

The state often dictates what is to taught and in what sequence. The state approves textbooks with titles such as *Algebra I, World History,* and the like. No publisher who expected to stay in business would issue texts intended for adoption in public education with titles such as *Getting Ready for Careers* or *Financial Stability in Tomorrow's World* or *How To Be A Life-long Learner.* But I'd wager concerned parents and employers would buy them for their young accomplished-citizens-to-be.

Humans tend to do what is EXpected of them. We know what is expected of us by what we are INspected for and what we are REspected for. If teachers are ever formally or informally evaluated (inspected-for), it is usually based on their knowledge of a particular subject-matter. Teachers are paid more for number of academic degrees (respected-for) than some other measure such as their performance in producing student accomplishments.

We are all heir to the paradigm of subject-matter-based educational content and design. We have had no other model. It does not seem to register with us that what we learned in school has not had, by and large, sufficient relevance to and influence on the serious matter of earning a living and coping with the business of everyday life. We are usually dumped into the post-education world ignorant of the knowledge and skills most needed and needed most frequently. This forces us to acquire the needed knowledge on our own or to learn by trial and error and/or from the benevolence of a mentor. Yet many of us continue to defend the subject-matter-based content we learned.

Early and constant conditioning is powerful. We are badgered by our parents and teachers that learning subject-matter is the key to a magic kingdom. We readily accept myths (at least over-generalizations) such as "calculus teaches you how to think," "Latin helps you learn English better," "people who don't know history are doomed to repeat it," "knowledge is power," "you never know when you might need it."

Public service spots in the media have role models propagandizing on the matter. The President of the United States beats the drums for "Education 2000" whose goals stress acquisition of subject-matter. For example, Goal 3 of Education 2000 is: *Every student will master English, mathematics, science, history, and geography...* (To be fair, there is some acknowledgment in the goals relating to *responsible citizenship* and *productive employment* and *life-long learning*, but these seem to be tacked-on as an afterthought. Or perhaps to appease some pragmatist on the committee.)

We are all under the strong influence of the subject-matter paradigm, but one segment of society is becoming somewhat vocal in its concern about the poor preparation of the young, the employer. In survey after survey, employers of new-hires cite deficits in reading comprehension, basic math, oral communication, work ethic and so forth. They complain about the large expenditure required for testing and interviewing thousands to find hundreds and/or the large outlay to remediate new hires. These employers do not expect the educational system to produce workers accomplished at the particular jobs they will be doing, but expect them to have the entry knowledge, skills, and attitudes required to be able to learn the jobs. They expect them to be *ready* to be trained.

Employers also express great concern that the situation is particularly critical now and in the foreseeable future because of global competition and the rapidly changing nature of the business world. Employers state the rapidly changing world of work not only demands that the traditional knowledge and skills taught must be improved, but that new performance will be required even at the entry level.

In sum, I submit that *one* of the fundamental causes of the problems cited is the essence of education itself: **The derivation of content from a subject-matter base, and then teaching it only in that context.** Why this results in non-accomplishment for many students is presented in the next chapter.

Among the numerous possible causes of problems in education, I believe the second most important is the **lack of skills and knowledge among educators concerning how to produce learning in their students.** Not only do teachers tend to teach what they've been taught, it seems they tend to teach HOW they've been taught. Again, how the content was presented when the teachers were students serves as an early and constant model for their current efforts.

In the last 25 years considerable progress has been made in research and development of techniques for teaching and learning. There are now known methodologies which have been shown to be highly effective in promoting the acquisition of knowledge and skills. There are also documented ways of increasing student motivation.

These developments have been implemented mostly in business, industry, and military organizations. I called this *Instructional Science* in a previous chapter. Unfortunately, not a great deal of

Instructional Science has found its way into public education. For the most part, teaching progresses much the same as it always has: Teachers lecture and occasionally demonstrate; students listen and occasionally are asked to do something; students are assigned homework; students take quizzes and exams to determine the degree learning occurred; students are sorted into A's, B's, C's, D's, and F's, depending on the *student's* efforts.

Writing in the *Harvard Educational Review* (Spring 1996), Richard Elmore of Harvard Graduate School of Education states:

> *We can produce many examples of how educational practices could look different, but we can produce few, if any, examples of large number of teachers engaging in these practices...*

If a given student for a given subject-matter does not do well, it is usually attributed to one or more of these characterizations of the *student*:

- *He didn't study/listen/make the effort.*
- *She is below average intelligence.*
- *He lacks ability in math/science/languages etc.*
- *She has a learning disability.*
- *He doesn't know how to learn.*
- *She is disadvantaged/has low motivation/has low self-esteem.*

Although any one or combination of the above might or might not be so, the point I'm trying to make: It rare that anyone ever talks about the *teacher's* effort/intelligence/ability/motivation etc. Schools are quick to take at least some of the credit for student achievements as measured by grades, honors, college acceptance, advanced placement and the like. So be it. However, must they not also accept some of the responsibility when the student does NOT achieve?

Perhaps I seem to be coming down hard on teachers. Teachers are not the cause of societal problems, except to the extent they are members of society and must, like all of us, share in the responsibility. It would be a serious over-generalization to infer from what I'm saying that teachers are solely to blame for non-accomplishment by the student. By and large, the majority of the teachers I've had and have known as a parent and have worked with professionally were dedicated and hard-working. Most labor under physical, political, and financial aversives many of us would not tolerate in our professional lives. There have been a few exceptions, but the vast majority of teachers I've known were by no means dumb or guilty of punishable malpractice. However, we must make the discrimination between "dumb" and "ignorant." Ignorance can be remedied by re-education.

Teachers are the key to improvement in the effectiveness of education, given that the stakeholders provide the major input to the base for content. The teacher must be the ringleader of the conspiracy for student accomplishment.

Education is a labor-intensive business. Currently we spend nearly 90% of educational budget on labor cost. Teachers salaries account for a good share of this. In Eden, the teacher is the conspiracy ringleader. To improve education we must improve teaching. Instructional Science focuses on the *teacher's* action as it *affects* learning.

There is a long list of other possible contributing causes of problems in education. Many of these have societal root-causes. It is not the teacher's fault that children present themselves with scant vocabularies, under-nourished bodies, and unstimulated cognition. Present day teachers are not responsible for the large percent of children from single-parent homes. They cannot be blamed for the alarming rate of teen pregnancies or for rampant illegal drug use. Violence is generally not something kids learn from teachers. To the degree that genetics plays a role in behavior of students (and the issue is by no means settled), the teacher can do nothing about it directly.

Teachers do not have ways to eliminate these contributing causes, but we must give them ways to *minimize the effects* of these root-causes. How to do this is becoming clearer. It must be made clear to teachers.

In summary, of the long list of possible contributing causes of problems, I am saying the three root-causes discussed are among the important ones and must be solved:
1. **Subject-matter-based curriculum content**
2. **Inadequate instruction**
3. **Low student motivation**

SOLUTIONS

If solutions must match the cause, then three macro interventions are indicated:
1. **Derive content (WHAT-is-taught) from a goal driven, accomplishment base.**
2. **Improve instruction (HOW it-is-taught).**
3. **Influence student motivation.**

The most dramatic of the three solutions above is the first. Taken literally, the entire complexion of the K-12 curriculum could change in a seemingly radical way if we were to start from an accomplishment base as opposed to the familiar subject-matter base for deriving content of formal schooling. Like the educators in Medianville, almost everyone holds to the paradigm of subject-matter-based instruction. I believe the shifting away from subject-matter as the base for content is an absolute must if we are to finally precipitate effective educational reform. In order to make the shift to an accomplishment base, we must first realize there is a strong case against subject-matter-based education.

6. The Case Against Subject-Matter-Based Education

The term base implies foundation. It indicates the starting place. The traditional starting place for education is the specification of content from a subject-matter base.

This traditional base of education organizes knowledge/ skills/information into gross segments such as algebra, history, physics, geography etc. I am proposing a different base for derivation of content of curricula: desired student accomplishments derived from analysis of educational goals.

When we suggest an accomplishment-based approach to deriving content of curricula, it is often erroneously interpreted to mean we don't teach knowledge. Such an interpretation is absurd. **We advocate teaching facts, concepts, principles, and information. However, we derive the content so that it will be directly RELEVANT and VALUABLE to the forestated goals of education. We do this by working backward from the base of desired post-educational accomplishments.**

What is true: We don't *start* the process of deriving educational content based on the traditional organization of knowledge by categories of subject-matter; and, we don't make any assumptions at the start of the redesign process about what will be taught.

The traditional base (starting point) for deriving content of curricula is: *What general subject-matter areas are there?* If one proceeds from a subject-matter base, then the specific content of the curriculum will be organized into gross categories such as history, math, grammar, chemistry etc. The next likely question would be: *What knowledge is there WITHIN each subject-matter area?* That is, what are the concepts, principles, and facts of chemistry? What are the concepts, principles, and facts of algebra? etc.

There is a great deal of difference between the answers we get when we ask, *What is there to know in each subject-matter category?* and when we ask *What is the most relevant and valuable to know to produce the desired accomplishments?*

Subject-matter-based education is such an old and well-entrenched paradigm even the more radical of educational reformers accept it as the base. As stated, the typical call for educational reform concentrates on redesign of elements concerning how-to-teach, not what-to-teach. As will be discussed later in this book, revision of how-to-teach is certainly needed, but we must derive content *before* addressing how to improve instruction. Instructional Science can produce learning of information whether it is of low value or high value. And, it costs as much or more also.

Subject-matter connotes a grouping of increments of knowledge under some general heading. For example, *physics* is a grouping of what is known about matter and energy and their interactions. Any general grouping could be broken down into sub-increments. Physics, for example, might be sub-categorized into *mechanics, optics, acoustics, heat, electricity, magnetism, radiation, atomic structure* and so forth. Each of these might be further sub-divided into more specific increments. For example, *electricity* might be divided into topics such *current* and *resistance*.

Ultimately, we could get down to individual pieces of knowledge and associated vocabulary such as: *Current may reverse its direction at regularly occurring intervals*, and *a potential difference of one volt produces a current of one ampere*, and scores more.

The present state of the art of Instructional Science is such that we could then teach this knowledge to a large majority of students to a high degree of acquisition, if we held instructional time and cost constant. But time and cost are relevant variables. We do not have unlimited time and money to teach everybody everything, even though we argue we have the instructional methodology to do so. But I must say again: **If it is not worth teaching, it is not worth teaching well.**

If we start with the purpose of education as *to teach students knowledge of various subject-matters,* any one of the gross traditional categories of subject-matter, or even many of their sub-sets, could occupy the lifetime of a person as a student. Even if we spent a lifetime in learning, all that is known today would still not be acquired. (Is there anyone in any given field who purports to know everything that is known about that field? If so, it would be a very small acreage.)

Couple the massive amount of currently known content with the fact that knowledge in many fields is doubling ever few years, then the impossibility/impracticality of the achieving the subject-matter purpose is apparent.

The traditional reaction to this dilemma has been to try to come to grips with and teach the "basics" in K-12, and reserve subsequent education for ever-increasing specialization in some subject-matter. An obvious example of this is medicine with its fragmentation into specialties, sub-specialties, and sub-sub specialties ad infinitum. The current explosion of information makes this true of most other fields as well.

As far as the basics are concerned, I ask: Basic to WHAT? The answer invariably comes back relating to the subject-matter categories, not to some approximation of the goals of education I suggested previously in this book.

The second difficulty involves: How well does subject-matter-based education work? The quick answer is "not very well" *even when measured against the traditional subject-matter acquisition goals.* (As evidence, review the data previously offered concerning test scores, literacy, etc.)

Interventions such as smaller classes, computers in the classroom, increase in teacher pay, site-based management, and higher standards have not had dramatic results, and usually cost a bundle.

If we assess how well subject-matter-based instruction works against educational goals expressed in accomplishment terms (*work preparation, citizen preparation* etc.), then the news is worse than "not very well," it is alarming.

As far as I can tell, no universal authority has decreed knowledge must be organized by bodies of subject-matter. I don't know who first tried to bring semblance of order to the physical and cognitive universes by designating knowledge into sets such as philosophy, math, art, history and so forth, but they didn't do us any favor for the purposes of educational design.

As new explanations of phenomena and new thought came about from discovery and reasoning, it became necessary to create additional categories of subject-matter such as psychology, economics, aerodynamics, etc. And, new ideas and processes precipitated the need for sub-sets within the subject-matter domains such as American literature, atomic physics, electronics etc.

I suppose it was natural with the advent of formal schooling people would mirror the organization-by-subject-matter as the model for organizing the content of education. How useful is this model for organizing knowledge?

It is not a matter of correct vs. incorrect, but useful vs not useful. My thesis is that subject-matter organization is not very useful IF one subscribes to my offered purpose and goals of education. That is, subject-matter-based instruction is less useful to the goal of influencing students to become accomplished citizens.

Over the last 20 years many of us who have worked in business, industry, and military have departed from subject-matter-based education as a way of influencing employee performance. My own paradigm-shift began to occur when we followed up graduates of courses whose content was subject-matter-based. The evaluation of post-instruction performance showed very disappointing results when work outputs and actions were assessed. In a shocking number of cases, NO on-the-job improvement occurred as a result of extensive and expensive educational interventions. That is, the content learned did not transfer from the instructional situation to the post-instructional world. Money and human capital were invested for scant return at best.

We found one of the causes of this failure to transfer information taught to the job situation was a misdiagnosis of the need for an educational type of intervention in the first place. Often some intervention other than instruction should have been prescribed, such as better incentives or better equipment or more efficient work processes. However, even when an instructional intervention was appropriate, no significant change in the post-instruction performance was seen in an unacceptable number of cases. One of our clients used the analogy: *We emptied our educational budget teaching principles of aerodynamics, but they couldn't fly the plane.* (I do not credit this quote in order to protect my source from corporate criticism.)

We surmised one of the main reasons for this failure was the use of an inappropriate base for deriving the content to be instructed. Industry/business/military instructors tended to model their courses after formal education's subject-matter-based approach when deciding content. If the instructional developers and instructors were dealing with some knowledge/skill need they tended to address what-to-teach by first asking: *What SUBJECT is applicable here?* Then, they progressively broke down the subject into more and more detailed increments of knowledge and skills within the topic. The sub-sets became "units" within a course.

The course title often reflected its subject-matter base. For example, if the students to be influenced were in management, then courses such as *Management Theory* tended to result. Nuclear power plant employees would be dipped into subject-matter vats such as *Principles of Thermodynamics*. Customer service workers were presented *Communication Theory*. Persons aspiring to jobs in the comptroller department would be liberally doused with *Economics*.

Two of the more extreme examples I ever saw: Entry-level military enlisted personnel took *Principles of War*. In a curriculum for hairdressers, *Human Anatomy and Physiology* was the centerpiece of the instruction.

The basic issue is
TRANSFER

It should be made clear the problem I am concerned with is the content in subject-matter-based courses does not transfer sufficiently to the job situation. That is, what the student is taught does not get used on the job after instruction. Obviously, if something is not taught at all, there will be no transfer.

The fail-to-transfer problem implies a bias: **For education to be valuable, it must be directly useful the POST-educational lives of students.** In other words, one of the main ways we determine the value of education is in terms of the degree of transfer. This is why the previously stated purpose and goals of education are stated in terms of the post-educational lives of students, not just in terms of knowledge acquisition. If one does not subscribe to such as the prime purpose of education, then my subsequent arguments are not very meaningful.

My insistence that usefulness-equals-transfer falls on receptive ears of business/industry/military leadership because formal instruction for job holders encumbers over $100 billion a year. Many leaders of organizations are no longer willing to tolerate such an outlay without some evidence the return at least equals the investment. The hard-nosed business leader does not tolerate instruction for its entertainment value only. The practical leader might like to believe in "learning for learning sake," but will not pay for it in today's highly competitive business environment.

Business folk are beginning to understand that return is obtained from instruction ONLY when it positively impacts job-performance. It is remarkable to me the sponsors in the business world never insisted on evidence of relevance and transfer before. I suppose early and constant conditioning about subject-matter-based content impacted the business person also.

For the general case in business, subject-matter-based instruction does not transfer sufficiently to justify the cost. We have case after case where a pound of subject-matter resulted in an ounce of transfer. Speaking only for myself, I suggest the same is generally true for public education, as it now stands, where over $300 billion is out-laid annually for K-12 instruction.

Reasons for
NON-TRANSFER

Why is subject-matter-based education so disappointing when viewed in terms of failure to transfer? I think there are three major interlocking reasons.

The first reason is: **Some students don't pay sufficient attention to subject-matter-organized information because of the perception it is not relevant or not important.**

At the macro level, from the way humans perceive it, the world is organized in sub-sets of different "lives." We live a life as a worker. We have a family life. We are members of a society. We all have an inner life. I believe humans seek to see how a given piece of information fits into one or more of these categories. If a piece of information does not readily plug in, it is more apt to be rejected as *not relevant* or *not important,* thus effort to learn and remember is decreased. Obviously, if the content is not learned and not remembered, information will have little opportunity to transfer to post-school life.

The weight given to relevancy and importance seems to increase as we get older. Adults tend to be much less tolerant than the young of information they can't see the relevance and value to one of their sub-lives. First graders will tolerate input of information of no obvious relevancy; but the tolerance for irrelevancy decreases over time. I think this is among the reasons why some kids grow more and more dispirited as they progress through the grades, and ultimately drop out when the law permits it.

Some teachers will suggest one should learn their subject-matter because it does, in fact, help in preparation for life. If this claim is not readily seen by the student or is contradicted by the student's experience, albeit limited, then a dissonance and tendency to distrust the teacher often occurs. This promotes a cynicism in some, and has a negative effect on the teacher's subject-matter in particular, and often on schooling in general.

I believe many students come to dislike (and therefore avoid) some subjects because they have a negative experience with it; and, part of the negative experience is the appearance of irrelevancy or low importance. It is difficult for a student to make the effort to learn, say, algebra when they've never seen anyone use it any time or in any place. (The need to solve a quadratic equation has never come up in my personal or professional life. I certainly couldn't recall how to do it if it ever does. I hope my life never depends on recognizing the ablative case. Does it come up in anyone's life except a Latin teacher or translator of old documents?)

Students tend to become cynical when history teachers promise an understanding of today's events by studying the past, yet all the students are asked to learn are endless lists of dates and names of foreign rulers. Math is touted to be the "handmaiden of science," but the trig teacher rarely consults with the physics instructor in any kind of conspiracy of coherence much less relevancy. (Is my mind a muscle? Is it now stronger somehow because I exercised it mightily to learn about sines and tangents?) It is not until college, or maybe graduate school, or maybe never the student sees that there is a relationship between biology and chemistry.

I think one of the fundamental causes of these things is the subject-matter paradigm for organizing knowledge. A given subject-matter becomes an end in itself with little relationship to other subject-matter sets, much less any relevancy to post-instruction life. Many teachers tend to lose themselves in their own subject-matter. The loss is ultimately the student's and perhaps society's.

Although teachers have various lives the same as their students, teachers have been taught to view relevancy in a different way. When information is organized by subject-matter, relevancy of a fact or concept according to teachers is usually viewed in context with the subject-matter category itself: *Is it important to the SUBJECT I'm teaching?*

Further, some teachers view relevancy of a particular piece of information as it relates to the further academics. How many times have we heard a teacher say, *You need to learn this because you'll need it when you study _____.*

Some students accept a sort of artificial relevancy when they attend to and study information because "it might be on the test," and thus linked to a grade, which becomes linked to short-term positive consequences such as parental praise and peer recognition. Some persist in learning because of the perception of a link to longer-term consequences such as SAT scores and college acceptance, and thus linked to a college degree which in some vague way will give them entry to the good life. That is a very long chain of events for many students. We propagandize students on the matter because we've been propagandized about it.

I suppose it could be said that one of the characteristics of a "good student" is long-term tolerance for irrelevancy. My son, for example, voiced to me much of his academic life the complaint that large amounts of the curriculum had little to do with his career and life aspirations, as far as he could tell. As far as I could tell also, but I tried not to bias him to this view, I promise you. I do recall telling him a big part of education was like getting a series of union cards to entitle him ultimately to work and live as he wanted. He seemed to buy that. He persisted and became an excellent student, as judged by traditional measures of grades, academic honors, and a couple of degrees in Electrical Engineering.

Later he told me: *Education is just learning words and messing around with numbers. I wish they had taught me how to use the words and numbers for something.* After securing his first a position with a large high-tech company at a shocking starting salary, he remarked to me: *I don't know how to be an engineer. I feel like a fraud.*

Even if students persist in learning, they tend to forget subject-matter-based knowledge because the potential relevancy is often not apparent to the student. (Except for passing tests and getting good grades and shocking starting salaries.) In fact, a considerable amount of knowledge taught in the traditional curriculum has, for all practical purposes, such remote potential relevancy it might be considered IRrelevant or UNimportant for the large majority of students, no matter how interesting it might be to the *teacher.* All subject-matters abound with these remote-chance-for-need pieces of knowledge—perhaps most of the content after about the fifth grade. (In cynical moments, possibly caused by low blood sugar, I sometimes think post-fifth grade schooling is mostly a holding place for kids until they get mature enough not to do too much damage to themselves and us.)

In addition to lack of attention by the student, there are additional penalties for teaching content of low-potential-relevancy. Student and teacher times are taken up when they could be better employed for content which has a higher potential for transfer. Teaching low-potential-relevancy information costs as much as high-potential content. Low-potential-relevancy information tends to make students cynical about content in general, thus they miss the opportunity to acquire the needed knowledge/skills/information.

The second reason subject-matter-based instruction fails to transfer to post-school life is that **content is not presented in a way that matches what the students will encounter post-school.**

At a more micro level, a large part of the lives of humans seems to happen in terms of *signals* and *actions*. A signal is presented to me. I do or think something following the signal. For example, I see a red traffic light. I think *red light means stop*. I step on the brakes. I see the written symbol *cat*. I think *kat*, and perhaps the mental image of a four-footed furry creature.

I have *learned* to associate these signals and actions previously. I was not born with information about decoding of written symbols and catness, nor was the important sequence brake-stepping-when-red-light-appears hard-wired in my brain at birth. I learn *best* when information is taught to me in that signal-action configuration and in that sequence. "Joe, when you see the letters *c-a-t*, think the sound *kat*. Here is a picture of one."

Further, I *apply* (do/think) the information best if the SAME signal or a very close approximation of it is presented to me again at a future time. What all this means is:

> **TRANSFER of information from education to post-school life occurs best when the signals and actions/thoughts taught in school MATCH the signals and required actions/thoughts that will occur POST-instruction.**

In other words, we increase the probability of transfer when the content of education resembles the post-instruction world as much as possible. (A considerable amount of data from brain and biochemical research is emerging to support this. If the reader is interested in an in-depth exploration of this topic, I suggest a good place to start is *How Brains Think* by William H. Calvin, 1996, BasicBooks, New York.)

The implication:

> **We should present content to the students and have them practice it as close as practical to the way they will see it post-school.**

Much subject-matter-based information is not presented in education in a signal-action sequence. Even on the occasion when the information is presented in signal-action sequence, often the signals and actions do not match the post-education situation close enough to allow the person to generalize (transfer) from the learning situation to the post-learning situation. Typically, information is just presented, and students exhorted to learn it:

- *Ohm's Law is...*
- *The types of cloud formations are...*
- *There are 12 cranial nerves...*
- *The Law of Supply and Demand is...*
- *Amo, amas, amat*
- *The major export of Brazil is...*
- *The Dodo is an extinct bird.*

On the job, the technician is not presented the signal, *What is Ohm's Law?* He/she is presented with a circuit where the resistance is unknown (signal), thus requiring the technician to measure the resistance (action). Though technically Ohm's Law is involved, would a student transfer this learning if taught only Ohm's Law? Can they fly the plane taught only principles of aerodynamics? Can I identify *E. histolytica* under the microscope, having been taught its life cycle and told stories about great amoebae the teacher has known?

Research, though scant on the matter, seems to show the brain tends to decode ("convert to meaning") information in a similar manner as it was encoded ("taught"). The difficulty is that the student is not called upon to recall subject-matter-based information like it was taught. That is, the post-instruction world presents signals different from what students experienced in education, requiring them to generalize before they can apply it. Study after study shows humans don't generalize well. Or said more pointedly, we don't teach them the content that will have a high probability of transfer, nor do we employ instructional methodology that will promote transfer.

The cynic might say that surely education should prepare us for more than an improbable appearance on a TV quiz show.

The third reason subject-matter-based instruction does not transfer is that **information learned will tend to be forgotten unless it is meaningful, exercised during the learning period, and exercised periodically thereafter.**

The issue here is: Unless knowledge is available in memory and can be retrieved, it will not be applied when needed. No one is certain exactly how information is stored and recalled. However, we do know the instructional tactics that will increase the probability of memory-storage.

Memory-storage seems to be affected by several things. Among the more important ones:

> *Meaningfulness of content.* Meaning*less* information is less likely to be attended to by the student in the first place. When the content IS meaningful, students will tend to concentrate on it for a longer period, thus increasing the probability of retention.

> *Amount of exercise during acquisition period.* Repetition during initial learning should occur until the student is fluent (correct and rapid). If students become fluent in a knowledge/skill, the rate of forgetting seems to decease. If not fluent, rate of forgetting tends to increase.

> *Level of reality of the exercise during acquisition.* As described above, the closer the signals-actions in the learning situation match the post-instruction situation, the more likely it is remembered as well as transferred.

> *Frequency of exercise AFTER initial learning.* Once something is learned it is not necessarily retained forever.

> Retention over time is greatly affected by how OFTEN the knowledge/skill is exhibited in the post-instruction situation. The more frequent the exercise, the greater the retention. On the other hand: **We tend to lose what we don't use**. It is difficult to increase the frequency of exercise of much of the content of traditional subject-matter-based education because the post-instruction world doesn't call for it. Supervisors do not give periodic exams on Ohm's Law. Quiz show appearance is very rare. The *E. histolytica* amoeba is almost never seen in the U.S.

All of us share a common experience: We were all educated from a subject-matter base. Somehow some of us developed a tolerance for irrelevancy to make the grades sufficient to obtain one or more union cards.

Some of us might be *accomplished citizens,* even by my presumptuous definition. Those who could be termed as such got that way somehow. Luck? Accident of birth? Genetics? A Divine plan? Trial and error? It would be arrogant of me to pretend I know the whole answer, but I'm afraid accomplishments in our post-instruction lives are not due in the main to the subject-matter we learned, at least not to the degree we propagandize students that it does. Knowledge in itself is not power. *Relevant* and *valuable* knowledge is power.

Assuming we cannot do much about many of the factors that positively influence accomplishments, I believe education could have a positive effect. But to have a positive effect we must dramatically improve education. I am trying to make the case in this book that a major tactic in improving education is by first adopting a different paradigm than subject-matter to decide WHAT is to be taught.

How, then, can we make education content more valuable for the student and society at large, more meaningful to the student, more likely to be transferred, and less likely to be forgotten? It starts by specifying the desired accomplishments as the base, and realizing there is a strong case for accomplishment-based education.

7. The Case for Accomplishment-Based Education

Work that is engaging to the student is almost always on some product or performance that is significant to them. The clearer the connection ... the more likely they will engage in the task.

–Philip C. Schlecthy
Inventing Better Schools

I've submitted there are three general causes of problems in education: The content taught does not transfer sufficiently; how the content is taught is not adequate even for the relatively less valuable purpose of teaching subject-matter; and, lack of student motivation.

I've attributed the lack of transfer in part to the traditional subject-matter base for curriculum content. That is, educators almost always begin by addressing the knowledge, skills, and information to be presented in the curriculum or any given course in the curriculum. And, the learning of this content becomes the only desired end.

The alternative to subject-matter-based derivation of content is *accomplishment-based* curriculum content. This means we specify the valuable post-instruction outputs before addressing relevant knowledge/skills/information (K/S/I) to be taught. The link between the desired accomplishments and the specific K/S/I to be taught are the processes relevant to the desired accomplishments.

The general model for accomplishment-based education:

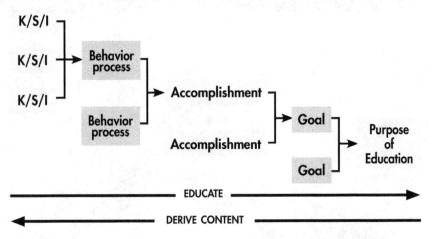

Education proceeds left to right. That is, we should teach knowledge/skills/information in order to influence students to be able to perform processes which result in accomplishments that are of value to the goals of education, which were derived from the agreed-on general purpose of education: *Produce graduates who have the skills, knowledge, information, and attitudes relevant to accomplished citizenship.*

We derive WHAT to teach by proceeding right-to-left. This increases the probability the content that is taught will be relevant, meaningful, and valuable to the general purpose.

Again, it is critical that we agree on the overall purpose of education in the beginning of the redesign effort. The key issue is whether we want education to influence students to become accomplished citizens, or to become merely knowledgeable in various subject matters.

Example of the relationship of the elements:

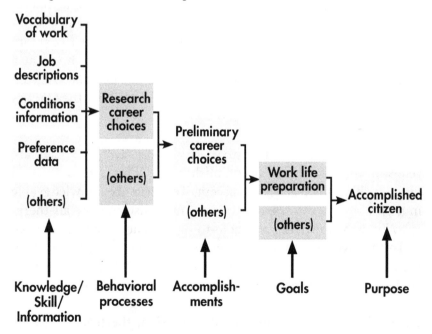

In the partial example above, the K/S/I are relevant to the processes, which are based on the accomplishments. Since there are four major goals, each consisting of major accomplishments, the number of behavioral processes and amount of specific K/S/I will be considerable. However, the content would be a small fraction of the universe of all known increments of knowledge/ skills/information. (Student attitude is a special case. Attitudes will be discussed at length in a later chapter.)

As stated, irrelevant or low-worth content takes up as much time as relevant and high value K/S/I. Since the amount of knowledge in any given subject-matter is very large, teachers will tend to attempt "coverage" of as much of it as they can in the relatively short time frame they have. Even holding relevancy and value constant, teachers then do not have time to engage in teaching activities which increase the probability of learning and retention of the K/S/I. Nor is there time to do much responding to individual differences in students. With good motives, some teachers present a topic and move on to the next and then the next in a frantic race with the clock and calendar. There is usually insufficient time to present elements to be learned in relatively small increments, obtain active responses from the students, allow students to explore examples of application of the topic, practice the content at a sufficient level of reality to help to promote fluency and transfer, give immediate feedback to the student, and all the other tactics we know which aid learning and transfer.

The solution I suggest is to derive those K/S/I which are relevant to the desired accomplishments. This seems to be a difficult thing for teachers to accept. Teachers are knowledgeable in their subject-matters; they often cannot discriminate all-there-is-to know from what is valuable-to-know. Their teachers did not make the discrimination. The teachers and their teachers usually became educators in the first place because they fell in love with a subject-matter. We tend to teach what and how we've been taught.

Given the traditional purpose of education, the teacher has no true basis for discriminating relevancy and importance of content. They, like their teachers, become lost in the large and dense forest of subject-matter. And, after all, this is what teachers were hired to do in the first place.

I suggest derivation of content from a purpose-goals-accomplishments-behavioral processes sequence is preferable for these overlapping reasons:

1. **Increased value and relevancy of K/S/I learned.**
   If it is true that at the bottom line it is the accomplishments that are valued, then K/S/I ultimately derived from a purposeful, goal-driven, accomplishment base would be more valuable because the content would be directly relevant to the behavioral processes that produce the accomplishments. Similarly, the specific K/S/I taught are likely to be more relevant because they are derived from behavioral processes that are relevant to goal-relevant accomplishments. This also gives the teacher a basis for discriminating between all-there-is-to-know and valuable-to-know.

2. **Increased attention and effort by the student.**
   Content would be more meaningful to the student as well as to the stakeholders in education. If the content is perceived as meaningful, the chances are increased the student will attend to the instruction in the K/S/I; and, perhaps increase the probability the student will expend energy to cooperate with the teacher to learn the content. This motivation to expend effort to learn increases the chances of acquisition of the content.

3. **Allows more in-depth learning.**
   Because the universe of content is likely to be narrower in scope, it is more practical to teach the K/S/I so that the student becomes fluent. The curriculum would not have to cover as much territory in the time traditionally allotted to K-12. The more the student is fluent in the learning, the greater the probability of the accomplishments. This means that the teacher must abandon "coverage" as the objective in favor getting the student to be fluent as the desired end. Less quantity, more quality, so to speak.

4. **Increases probability of transfer**

   If content is irrelevant, it obviously will not transfer because there is no situation to transfer to. If the content is of low-potential-relevancy, the frequency of post-instruction need, and therefore use, will be low. If the frequency of use is low, decrease in retention will occur. Infrequent exercise is a prime cause of lack of retention.

   K/S/I derived from behavioral processes are more likely to be configured in signals-actions; consequently, transfer will be more likely. Also, it is more likely the K/S/I will get more frequent exercise because the post-educational world exercises signals-action. The need for the student to make a long chain of generalizations from the instructional situation to post-school application would be reduced. The simple fact is: Most humans, on their own, do not generalize well.

5. **Illuminates the need for meaningful basic skills.**

   Basic skills are defined as that content which underlies and facilitates the acquisition of future skills. Since the "future skills" will be specified in the goals-accomplishments-behavioral process progression, we can more easily determine what the *common* and appropriate facilitating skills are—the basics; and, perhaps teach many of them in the primary years of education.

   These basic skills are, of course, likely to include reading and dealing with numbers, but could include such non-traditional basic skills such as oral expression, keyboarding, listening, and the like. By deriving the basic skills from the goals-accomplishments-behavioral processes-S/K/I progression, even these "generic" skills can be made more meaningful for the student. For example, the local newspaper could be used even in the early primary years as one of the vehicles for teaching and practicing obvious basic skills such as reading, but could also be used to begin the introduction of, and laying the groundwork for, skills such as discriminating fact from claims, recognition of main points in written materials, making informed decisions about purchasing etc.

6. **Allows for more meaningful evaluation of learning.**
In traditional approaches to education the method for assessment is a test which usually seeks to determine the recall of facts relevant to some sub-set of a subject. Often, this is a multiple-choice exam. In math, and sometimes in science, the exam might call for the student to work a problem or explain an operation. This is fine as far as it goes. When the specific behavioral processes are known and taught, then assessments would seek to determine the students can DO/ THINK as a result of the instruction, not just what they "know." In addition, since the desired outputs of instruction in my scheme are accomplishments, long-term measurement of value is rendered more probable.

A considerable number of the growing legion which calls for reform of education suggest we must "get back to basics." When one examines what they propose, it is NOT a change in base being recommended. Often the back-to-basics suggested is to concentrate on more "core knowledge" because, it is suggested, new knowledge is formed on prior knowledge. While the statement is certainly true, my question is still: *Knowledge for what end?* It is the ends (purpose, goals, accomplishments) which form a different base.

Similarly, there is sometimes a confusion about what we mean when we call for deriving content from an accomplishment base. It is often misintrepreted to mean we first decide to populate the curriculum with theory, concepts, principles, and facts of some subject-matter, then give examples of how these might be used or "applied." The opposite is true: *We first look for the performance that is valuable, then determine what information is needed to facilitate it.* That is, we must follow this sequence and no other:
A. **Based on goals, what should they accomplish?**
B. **What should they learn to do and/or think to produce the accomplishments?**
C. **What specific K/S/I must they learn to facilitate #B?**

Is accomplishment–based same as
outcome–based?

It has been suggested there seems to be a relationship between my accomplishment-based education philosophy and the outcome-based movement of the early '90s. The main similarity is that both deal with "ends." However, in much of the outcome-based education I've seen, the ends are usually very general and open to wide interpretation. Examples:

- *Students shall interpret relationships, patterns and connections among a variety of phenomena.*
- *Articulate the interdependence among social systems.*
- *Recognize patterns and cause-effect relationships common in history.*

These seem intellectual and somehow important, but what could those possibly mean? I submit even if we could agree on meanings, the most advanced thinkers in the world would struggle to do those things. Noted historians, for example, vainly struggle to "show patterns and cause-effect relationships common in history." Besides, what value to the educational goals that I've proposed would these be anyway? It is not obvious to me on the face of the examples I've seen.

Contrast the examples of outcomes above with these examples of accomplishments:

- *Students will be able to produce a schedule for use of their time.*
- *...a preliminary decision concerning career path.*
- *...interpretation of food labels.*
- *...obedience to traffic laws.*
- *...interpretation of news articles*

Also, there has been some organized opposition to outcome-based education which I fear will bleed over to accomplishment-based education. Reading the literature concerning the opposition, I conclude the objection is not to the idea of stating desired outcomes per se, but because the outcomes produced were often nebulous. Also, many of the outcomes suggested dealt with values and potential content the opposers do not want, or believed should not be in the province of the school. For example: sex education, diversity, self-esteem, tolerance for ambiguity, morals and the like.

Part of the opposition also seems to stem from certain other controversial issues that have become somehow identified with outcome-based education such as: changes in testing and grading; diminishing competition among students; mainstreaming of special-education students; ungraded primary schools, use of computers in teaching.

The *possible* accomplishments should be made as clear and as detailed as possible. Then, those the stakeholders desire to be influenced by education should be identified by consensus of the community. I am not so naive to believe reaching an agreement will be easy, but illumination of the issues and alternatives is the first step toward that end.

Accomplishment-base education and "intellectualism"

The general idea that education should prepare students for the "real world" is not a new one. (An accomplishment-base for education is, however, new.) The idea cropped up periodically over the last 150 years in one form or the other. It seems to have appeal to the proverbial man in the street. Given this appeal to the so-called ordinary citizen, it is often condemned as "anti-intellectual" by those whose lives are occupied largely with a subject-matter. This includes many philosophers, academicians, writers, and social commentators.

When I ask those who voice the anti-intellectual opposition to the accomplishment-based paradigm to tell me who are the models for intellectualism they want students to emulate, they usually list names of fellow philosophers, academicians, writers, and social commentators. I am not implying that philosophers, academicians, writers, and social commentators should be dismissed. I am simply saying Descartes, the head of an Ivy League English department, a Nobelist in poetry, or a William Buckley are not necessarily the only, or even the prime, role models for the accomplished citizen. Consulted? Yes. Emulated in terms of their subject-matter base? No.

When I push further concerning the opposition, I often find there has been the over-generalization I cautioned against earlier: the incorrect assumption that we do not teach facts, concepts, principles, verbal information, and "big ideas." This is in no way true. Again, it is the base and process for deriving content that are different.

I stand foursquare FOR intellectualism. I've spent a good portion of my life in formal settings learning subject-matter. I've been an academician. I read in a wide range of disciplines, some in considerable depth. I simply enjoy knowing. I can bore friends with arcane information about the Aztec and the Zulu. I've read all of Hardy, Tolstoy, and even Pynchon. I believe I can argue either side of the debate between Skinnerians and Rogerians. My home library is crammed with treatises on history, linguistics, and science tomes. I pepper my speech with Latin. I even know the names of Millard Fillmore's cabinet.

But those things have little to do with what I did last week in any direct way: negotiated with a dealer for a new car; analyzed whether it is better to buy or lease; interpreted some physical symptoms I experienced; counseled my son on a career decision; satisfactorily settled a disagreement with my wife; and outlined the main points of this chapter. These valuable things I accomplished last week had precious little to do with the 20 years of formal subject-matter-based education I sat through, certainly with the latter 12 or 13 of those years.

Many years after completing the same doctoral curriculum, several of us sat around recalling that indignant experience. We decided to make a list of the K/S/I learned in the courses which had a modicum of utility to our subsequent professional lives. After being able to come up with only a few things in statistics and probability, we abandoned that fruitless game and spent the rest of our reunion time gossiping.

I don't believe in withholding any facts, concepts, principles, and information from anyone. I believe that institutions and curricula built around study of the "Great Books" should survive. I think students should have access to any subject-matter in which they are interested. I think people should become philosophers, academicians or writers or social commentators if they choose. But it is absurd and unworkable to cite what these subject-matter specialists know as THE model for the content of public education for everyone.

By the same token, I think it is a crime against the young and society not to deal directly with the knowledge/skills/information that have direct bearing on the opportunity to become accomplished citizens. That base is a matter of definition by ALL the stakeholders, not just the philosopher or the academician or even this commentator.

What Accomplishments? What Behavior?

Given we want to determine the specific content to be taught by retrogressing from purpose and goals, the pivotal elements are the accomplishments subordinate to each general goal.

Accomplishment: *An output a human produces that has value to a particular goal.*

Statements of accomplishments always begin with a noun or noun modifier such as an adjective or an article.

In business/industry/military education the specification of desired accomplishments depends on the occupation or profession to be influenced

For example, the desired major accomplishments of a *salesperson* might be:
- A list of qualified prospects
- A plan for contacting prospects
- Orders for the product
- A satisfied customer after problems with the product
- A plan for follow-up of unsuccessful sales efforts

We judge a salesperson by these outputs.

Desired major accomplishments of a physician's *office nurse* might be:
- Patients ready for treatment
- Treatments from physicians' orders
- Patients who can perform required home procedures
- Answers to patients' questions
- Emergency treatments in absence of physicians

Desired major accomplishments of a *nuclear reactor operator* might be:
- An evaluation of current status of the plant
- Decisions regarding change in the condition of the plant
- The plant ready for refueling
- The plant at normal condition after unsafe condition
- The plant secure after potential or actual emergency

For each major accomplishment, we could then derive the behavioral processes required to produce each output. For each behavioral process we could then derive the specific knowledge/skills/information needed to perform the process.

Public education is not, and should not be, devoted to preparing students for a particular occupation except in the broad sense that being an *accomplished citizen* is the target "occupation" for all students. Thus, the analog for public education are the "sub-occupations": potential worker, society member, family member, and individual. For example, in the student role of *potential worker* one of the major accomplishments might be *preliminary career choice*. For the role of *individual* one of the targeted accomplishments might be *stable financial condition*.

I believe all stakeholders in education (parents, employers, teachers, and other members of the community), should have an input to the content of education in the sense they are the customers of the "product" of education. If so, then the stakeholders should decide the desired accomplishments.

Over the last several years I've collected examples from various constituencies concerning their wants in regard to desired accomplishments and behavioral processes. I used the previous macro-goals to provide some structure and focus for the effort. For example, if the group surveyed was made up of potential employers, they were asked to provide examples of entry expectations for job candidates. If they were parents, they were asked to describe outputs and behaviors relating to becoming accomplished family members. I queried all groups concerning society membership as a whole.

Though I've sampled several hundred citizens, I do not suggest my surveys were scientific or complete. I do not suggest these particular accomplishments are the most valuable ones. I merely relate examples of their desired accomplishments below to illustrate the idea of the base for deriving specific content of education.

Examples of desired ACCOMPLISHMENTS for the *potential worker:*
- A preliminary decision concerning career choice
- A decision regarding formal schooling needed for career
- Preparation for seeking employment
- Interpretation of work-related written materials
- Written work-related messages
- Interpretation of spoken messages from others
- Communication of oral messages
- Work-related calculations and estimations
- Work ethic and commitment to quality
- Work-appropriate dress, personal hygiene, and grooming
- Freedom from illegal chemical substances
- Cooperation and resolution of conflict with supervisors and peers
- Cooperation when working on a team

Examples of desired accomplishments for the *individual:*
- A plan for life-long acquirement of knowledge and skill
- Acquisition of prerequisites for life-long learning
- A healthy body
- Stable personal financial condition
- Control of emotions and stress
- A tolerance for individuals and other cultures
- Information from references
- The avoidance of addictions
- Information and pleasure from general reading
- Informed purchase decisions
- A plan for use of time
- Clothing in proper condition
- Interpretation of legal documents
- "Devil's Advocacy" regarding claims

For *society member:*
- Obedience to the law
- An informed voting decision
- Interpretation of news, current events, and socio-political issues
- Contributions to stable environment
- Social interaction
- Resolution of conflict with other members of society
- Decisions regarding societal issues
- A tolerance of cultural differences
- Proper public comportment, ethics, and manners
- Access to community services
- Contributions to community improvement

For *family member:*
- Decisions regarding marriage and procreation
- Healthy, safe, and developed children
- A safe home environment
- A nutrition plan for the family
- Meals
- Oral communication with family members
- The resolution of conflict with family members
- A stable family financial condition
- Decisions regarding insurance
- Decisions regarding housing
- Decisions regarding transportation
- Decisions regarding purchases and financing
- Care of the elderly
- Maintenance and repair of property

It is difficult for all of us to avoid thinking in terms of the subject-matter model for organizing the universe of knowledge. The ultimate organization of knowledge/skills/information by accomplishment represents a very different schema. It is likely to be uncomfortable at first. At least that was our experience when we employed it for deriving content in the business, industry, and military education arenas. We were unable to get some to make the paradigm-shift. When we were able to convince organizations to employ a goal-driven, accomplishment-based progression, several major benefits resulted. Because development of educational courses is costly, an immediate noticeable benefit was reduced development time. One reason this occurred was because it was easier to get agreement among stakeholders in the educational projects on *what* would be taught. This efficiency comes about when specific content is the *last* issue to be addressed in the analysis phase. After leading the sponsors through the purpose-goal-accomplishment-behavioral process sequence, the specific knowledge/skills/information needed become relatively obvious. If one starts with the question *what do you want them to know?* lengthy discussions and debates ensue among the sponsors. This often results in an abundance of content to placate advocates of a particular subject-matter. Coming to an agreement on desired accomplishments was comparatively easy.

Another benefit which appealed especially to the cost-sensitive sponsor was shorter courses, compared to those based on a subject-matter model. This was due in part to the rifle-approach to deriving content. The volume of content was usually less because only the *relevant*-to-know knowledge/skill/information were emphasized in the courses. Subject-matter-based courses tend to be fatter because there is little basis for discriminating relevancy. With good motives, the instructors tried to pack in as much information as possible. They tried to achieve maximum "coverage."

In one instance we were able to reduce an 80-hour subject-matter-based course to four hours. Cutting course times in half was common. Eliminating some subject-matter-based courses altogether was also common. (When it was demonstrated the course content did not have much direct relevance to desired accomplishments.)

The biggest benefits realized were that the content was learned better by the student, and transferred to the job to a greater degree. (Reasons for this were discussed in the previous chapter—better motivation to learn, modeled after post-instruction situation, minimization of forgetting etc.)

Behavorial
Processes

Given agreement on the desired accomplishments of education, many people tend to jump to the question: What are the specific knowledge/skills/information needed to enable student to produce those outputs? We have found that a further specification is required before addressing the specific content to be taught: The *behavioral processes* students should learn how to DO in order to produce the outputs.

Recall that we are working in reverse of this general sequence...

S/K/I learned → Behavior process → Accomplishment → Goal → Purpose

In this context *process* means a series of steps. *Behavior* means the actions or thoughts of a human.

Behavioral process: *Actions and/or thoughts a human engages in that produces an output.*

Statements of a behavioral process always begin with a verb.

If we were dealing with an educational project for the job of physician's office nurse, examples of the behavioral processes might be:

Accomplishment: *Treatments from physician's orders*
Behavioral processes:
- *Remove sutures*
- *Dress wounds*
- *Give injections*
- *Give oral medications*
- *Give EKG*

Accomplishment: *Patient has information to perform home procedures*
Behavioral processes:
- *Instruct on home-care of diabetes*
- *Instruct on home-care of colostomy*
- *Instruct on home-care of wounds*
- *Instruct on breast self-examination*
- *Give information on side effects of medication*

In education we are not preparing students for specific occupations, but for their future roles as workers, family members, individuals, and society members. But we would still specify relevant behavioral processes. Examples of behavioral processes relevant to the student's accomplishments:
- *Sample various careers*
- *Deal with anger and stress*
- *Interpret legal documents*
- *Decide when to seek professional medical help*
- *Inspect home for safety*
- *Read for pleasure*
- *Create a budget*
- *Obey traffic laws*
- *Interact in a social situation*
- *Use and interpret references*

Is "thinking"
behavior?

An increment of behavior can be made up of mostly overt (observable) steps, or could be largely covert actions ("thinking"). Most behavioral processes are combinations of thinking and doing when described to a deep level of detail.

I raise the issue of covert/overt behavior because of a common misconception: Some have misconstrued that those of us who espouse teaching knowledge/skill/information relevant to behavioral processes don't deal with "thinking." This is nonsense. One need only look at the list of example behavioral processes above to see that covert behavior is dealt with. Verbs such as *decide*, *inspect*, and *interpret* indicate actions one cannot directly observe. *Reading*, for example, is all covert behavior. (Could one possibly suggest we would not teach reading?)

We *do* espouse: The *relevant* covert behavior be derived in the same manner as relevant overt behavior.

The examples of behavioral processes below for some of the accomplishments are for illustration purpose only. They are not necessarily complete or necessarily suggested to be included in the curriculum.

> **Role: *Individual***
> Accomplishment: *Information from references*
> Behavioral processes:
> * *Use the library*
> * *Use dictionary and thesaurus*
> * *Use manuals*
> * *Use electronic sources*

Accomplishment: *Stable financial condition*
Behavioral processes:

- *Discriminate needs and wants*
- *Create a budget*
- *Save for future needs*
- *Finance major purchases*

Accomplishment: *Healthy body*
Behavioral processes:

- *Engage in cardiovascular fitness activities*
- *Engage in muscular strengthening activities*
- *Follow nutritious diet*
- *Avoid contamination and harmful substances*
- *Care for minor ailments and injuries*
- *Decide when to seek medical help*

Accomplishment: *Control of emotions*
Behavioral processes:

- *Identify emotional and stress symptoms*
- *Deal with stress and anger*
- *Deal with depression*
- *Deal with jealousy*
- *Deal with impulses, obsessions, and compulsions*
- *Decide when to seek professional assistance*

Role: *Society member*
Accomplishment: *Informed voting decision*
Behavioral processes:

- *Gather relevant information from reading newspapers and magazines*
- *Gather relevant information from electronic media*
- *Gather relevant information from discussions with others*
- *Assess personal values and convictions regarding issues and candidates*
- *Weigh pros and cons of options against personal values and societal needs*

Accomplishment: *Obedience to the law*
Behavioral processes:
- *Obey driving and traffic laws*
- *Obey laws regarding alcohol and drugs*
- *Obey laws regarding bodily harm*
- *Obey laws regarding property*

Accomplishment: *Resolution of conflict*
Behavioral processes:
- *Avoid creation of situations of potential conflict*
- *Defuse anger and hostility*
- *Pinpoint conflict problems, causes, and solutions*
- *Negotiate and compromise*

Accomplishment: *Public comportment*
Behavioral processes:
- *Exhibit courtesy when driving*
- *Exhibit courtesy at public events*
- *Dress appropriately for occasions*
- *Use appropriate table manners*
- *Use appropriate language with others*

Role: *Family member*
Accomplishment: *Oral communication with family members*
Behavioral processes:
- *Decide purpose of message to be sent*
- *Encode messages*
- *Edit messages for intent and clarity*
- *Elicit feedback concerning comprehension*
- *Decode return messages*

Accomplishment: *Healthy, safe, and developed children*
Behavioral processes:

- *Care for the infant*
- *Develop cognitive and psychomotor skills in children*
- *Influence the values and motivation of children*
- *Recognize symptoms of childhood diseases*
- *Engineer a safe environment*

Accomplishment: *Decisions regarding housing*
Behavioral processes:

- *Allocate financial resources to housing*
- *Determine housing needs*
- *Weigh rent vs buy option*
- *Secure insurance*
- *Arrange for utilities*
- *Allocate spaces for functions*

Role: *Potential worker*
Accomplishment: *Preliminary decision concerning career*
Behavioral processes:

- *Gather information concerning work from written sources*
- *Observe and discuss jobs with current job holders*
- *Simulate behaviors of a sampling of jobs*
- *Inventory personal likes and dislikes*

Accomplishment: *Work ethic and commitment to quality*
Behavioral processes:

- *Commit to work-time parameters and deadlines*
- *Commit to organization rules and policy*
- *Plan use of time*
- *Stay on-task*
- *Commit to criteria of work outputs*
- *Inspect outputs for quality*

Accomplishment: *Work-related calculations and estimations*
Behavioral processes:
- *Estimate quantities*
- *Measure quantities*
- *Perform arithmetical operations*
- *Perform fundamental statistical operations*

Accomplishment: *Cooperation with supervisors and peers*
Behavioral processes:
- *Clarify assignments, deadlines, and criteria for outputs*
- *Ask for assistance from supervisor and peers*
- *Accept feedback*
- *Resolve conflicts with supervisors and peers*

One can begin to see the usefulness of having the specification of behavioral processes. They point the way to more rational decisions concerning the specific knowledge/skills/information needing to be taught. As discussed later in this book, behavioral processes organize content in such a way it makes curriculum design less arbitrary. They form the basis for more effective instruction and more meaningful evaluation of student learning.

The Eden Conspiracy

9. Deriving Knowledge/Skills/Information to be Taught

If the community is in a real sense the "customers" for education, then it is appropriate to consult them on matters relating to content of education.

Two of the principle stakeholders in education are parents and employers. I surveyed a considerable sample of both groups.

What content parents want taught

When I surveyed several hundred non-educators across the United States concerning what they thought important for kids to learn in the K-12 years, I was somewhat surprised they did not talk in subject-matter terms such as "a basic understanding of history," "two years of algebra," "college preparatory subjects." I was surprised because we are all conditioned by our formal schooling to think of content in terms of subject-matter categories.

Instead, parents typically responded with items compatible with the preparation-for-life theme of this book. Listed below in random order are the more frequent responses of parents.

• Organizing one's life	• Importance of good credit
• Distinguish right and wrong	• Finding a job
• Tolerance	• Decision making
• Seek compromise in conflicts	• Birth control
• Using time well	• Appreciation of art
• Study habits	• Respect for authority
• Delay of gratification	• Non-discrimination
• Benefits of saving	• Basic math
• Budgeting money	• Listening skills
• Getting along with others	• Speak in public
• Learning how to learn	• Orderliness
• Coping with change	• Work ethic
• Banking	• Good health habits

- Writing
- Conversing
- Respect for property
- Setting goals
- Persistence
- Completing tasks
- Map reading
- Respect for others
- Parenting skills
- Personal ethics
- Obedience to law
- Literature appreciation
- Importance of hygiene
- Nutrition
- Getting a meal together
- Negotiating
- Reading
- Concern for environment
- Self-control
- Selection of friends
- Effects of drugs
- Understand a contract
- Speaking grammatically
- Distinguish fact and opinion
- Adaptability

It is interesting to note that many of the items above relate to "attitudes" and "values" (e.g. *respect for authority, delay of gratification, persistence, ethics*) in contrast to the academic content we usually associate with formal schooling.

It could be argued many of the items above are the responsibility of parents or institutions such as religious organizations, not the schools. Perhaps so. That is an issue that must be debated and a consensus reached. Here I merely report what the constituency said. Like the citizens of Eden, my respondents seem to think of schools, the community, and maybe the family as certainly over-lapping, if not seamless.

The difficulty is that many students are NOT acquiring many of these K/S/I and attitudes anywhere. For example, the National Center for Financial Education says: *The biggest mistake parents make is to wrongly assume children are going to learn these things in school. There is no uniform program for financial education in schools.*

My everyday experience seems to support the suggestion by the parent stakeholder that the desired knowledge/skills/attitudes are not being exhibited in everyday life. Though every generation who has reached majority seems to decry the new one, current behavior of the young seems to be particular deficit. I am constantly being given incorrect change. I must wade through mumbles and utterances filled with *he goes like* (which I think means *he said*); *ya know what I'm saying* (no I don't); and the universal *whatever*. Sentences devoid of any approximation of standard grammar is the standard of many under the age of 50. Right vs wrong seems to be a discrimination impossible to grasp. Manners and respect seem to be quaint notions.

One could pass off my experience to the grumpiness of someone entering his autumn years, but the alarming statistics on drug use, teenage pregnancy, violence among the young and so forth seem to lend some support to my contention. Though it would be an absurd simplification to lay the entire blame of such societal problems on education, it surely suggests current education with its narrow emphasis on academic subject-matter is not effective to even minimize the effects very much.

What Employers Want
Taught

Survey after survey of employers supports the point that many of the entry K/S/I and attitudes required for employment are not present in a majority of the applicants and new-hires.

K/S/I frequently cited in our surveys of employers:

• Work ethic	• Oral presentations
• Staying on task	• Written communication
• Commitment to quality	• Using time well
• Problem solving	• Computer literacy
• Basic math	• Proper dress for job
• Team working	• Penmanship
• Cooperating with others	• Safe work habits
• Critical thinking	• Personal hygiene
• Avoiding drugs	• Using references
• Honesty	• Punctuality
• Keyboarding	• Respect for authority
• Estimating quantities	• Creative thinking
• Measuring	• Budgeting money
• Common sense	• Use appropriate language
• Accepting feedback	• Basic courtesy
• Reading directions	• Commitment to goals
• Listening	• Racial tolerance
• Controlling temper	• Conserve resources

Employers do complain about unsatisfactory preparation in the 3-Rs and obvious work-related skills such as *keyboarding* and *measuring*, but their concerns, like the parents, also involve attitudes and values the same as parents—*work ethic, honesty, racial tolerance, courtesy.*

Surveys conducted by The National Center on the Educational Quality of the Workforce in 1995 show far and away *good attitude* and *communication skills* are the most valued by employers when they hire employees. (Grades in academic subjects was far down the list.)

A Roper poll of employers in 1997 asked how well students were being prepared in work-related skills. Percentage who responded "very well":

Basic computer skills 14%
Work in diverse groups... 13%
Oral communications... 9%
Able to meet deadlines... 8%
Basic math skills.. 8%
Written communications 6%

I am struck by the employers' de-emphasis on the traditional vocational-technical skills such as clerical tasks, machine operating, troubleshooting, tool using. I surmise this is indicative of two things: the changing nature of jobs from manufacturing to dealing with information and services; and, the acceptance of employers that it is their responsibility, not the schools, to train new-hires for job-specific tasks. The often-quoted remark of David Kearns, CEO of Xerox illustrates the difference: *Business will train if schools will educate. No one needs to go to public school to learn how to repair a Xerox machine.*

Louis Gerstner, CEO of IBM, sums it up:

> *We can teach them what they need to know to run a machine or to develop a marketing plan. What is killing us is having to teach them to read, to compute.*

An example in support of Mr. Gerstner's point: When an American company wants to teach its employees statistical process control (an important skill now being widely implemented in industry), it will spend at least $200 per employee to teach it. If the employee does not have basic math skills, it costs as much as $2,000 per employee. This is in contrast to Japan who spends about $1 per employee to teach the same skill.

Deriving specific
content

It warrants repeating that one of the main reasons for retrogressing from overall purpose of education is to make the most important decision in education: WHAT to teach? I believe we should teach those increments of knowledge/skills/information and perhaps values/attitudes which increase the chances the student will perform the behavioral processes valuable to their post-instruction roles.

It also warrants repeating we should not make any undocumented assumptions about what-will-be-taught at the beginning of the educational reform process. One might comment that surely there are some basic skills such as the 3-R's we can assume, and therefore do not have to be derived out of the retrogression I propose. Though I'd bet on the probability that some aspect associated with the 3-R's would, in fact, show up when we do the analysis, it is the matter of assumption that is dangerous. When we begin to make assumptions then it might not ever stop. Soon, I fear, we might be swayed to accept all students should learn Latin, and all taught tap-dancing.

Given a behavioral process, the essential issue is: In specific terms, what do they need to learn in order to be able to do and think the overt and covert actions embodied in the process?

As can be seen by the aforementioned list, employers tend to suggest K/S/I synthesized in generic categories such as *problem-solving, critical thinking, common sense, planning.* I caution us on the tendency to revert back to subject-matter-like generalities at this point. For example, given the behavioral process, *communicate oral messages*, we might say they need a course on the theories of communication. Given the behavioral process, *identify emotional and stress symptoms*, we don't want to decree a course in psychology. Given the process *decide lease vs purchase*, there is a tendency to call for a course in decision making. Even though hairdressers deal with part of the body, we don't want to put them through instruction on human anatomy.

The employers' tendency to prescribe in subject-matter-like terms reveals to me the powerful grip subject-matter-based education has on us. Synthesizing by generic topics or "competencies" such as problem solving, decision-making, communications, critical thinking is only a step away from gross segments such as history, math, social studies etc. (Why teaching a generic topic or competency is not sufficiently effective is discussed below.)

Before we form categories of content, it is best to generate the specific increments of K/S/I to be taught, and the "basic skills" that are needed to support the content. That is, we should analyze (breakdown into parts) before we synthesize (put together into wholes).

Given the behavioral processes relevant to each accomplishment, we then address the supporting K/S/I required to perform the processes. Suppose, for example, we were doing a project in industrial education, and had this behavioral process that needed to be learned by students who were preparing to work in a nuclear power plant control room: *Monitor the control panel for indications of possible abnormalities.*

We'd then determine the specific K/S/I the students need to perform the overt and covert actions in an accomplished manner. For example, we might need to teach these specific things to support the behavior of control board monitoring:

- The meanings of the labels and symbols on each dial on the panel
- The meaning of the graduation markings on each dial
- The normal-value range of each dial
- The calculation required to determine abnormal trends
- The process for deciding if problem diagnosis is indicated

Given the content above, we could then examine each increment to decide if there are any basic skills required. For example, *calculations relevant to determining abnormal trends* might require teaching or refreshing the students on some specific (not all) aspect of statistics.

Suppose in another case we were developing a curriculum in a management education project and had this behavioral process relevant to some desired accomplishment: *Give feedback to a subordinate.* The specific K/S/I might be:

- Discrimination among types of feedback
- When to give each type of feedback
- Proper form and wording of each type of feedback
- Common responses of subordinates to feedback

Although public education is not the same as business and industry education, we might use the same kind of approach to derive the specific K/S/I needed. Examples:

Role: *Individual*
One accomplishment: *Information from references*
One behavioral process: *Use dictionary*
Example K/S/I:
- *Alphabetizing*
- *Estimating spelling of first syllables*
- *Meaning of diacritical marks*
- *Meaning of abbreviations used in dictionary*
- *Vocabulary used ("prefix," "synonym," etc.)*

Role: *Family member*
One accomplishment: *Healthy, safe, developed children*
One behavioral process: *Recognizing symptoms of childhood diseases*
Example K/S/I:
- *Vocabulary relevant to childhood diseases*
- *Common childhood diseases*
- *Usual symptoms of childhood diseases*
- *Consequences of untreated childhood diseases*
- *Discrimination of normal and abnormal states of children*
- *Taking temperature, pulse, and respiration of children*
- *Discrimination of when to seek professional aid*

Role: *Potential worker*
One accomplishment: *Preliminary decision concerning career*
One behavioral process: *Gather information on options*
Example K/S/I:
- *General categories of occupations and professions*
- *Examples of specific jobs in each category*
- *General nature of the work in each job*
- *General pros and cons of each job*
- *Educational preparation needed for each job*

Role: *Society member*
One accomplishment: *Informed voting decision*
One behavioral process: *Gather information from newspapers*
Example K/S/I:
- *Vocabulary relevant to newspapers*
- *Sections of a newspaper*
- *Discriminate a news story from an editorial*
- *Find news stories and editorials regarding voting issues*
- *Discriminate fact from opinion*

Given the content represented by the K/S/I increments, we could then examine them to determine the relevant basic skills needing to be taught to enable the students to acquire the content. Examples:
- Recognizing sounds of letters and syllables
- Decoding written words
- Recognizing meaning of words
- Spelling
- Pronouncing words
- Determining meaning of written phrases and sentences
- Analyzing grammar of a sentence
- Determining meaning of spoken sentences
- Speaking sentences
- Handwriting words and sentences
- Keying words, sentences, and paragraphs
- Recognizing numbers
- Adding, subtracting, dividing numbers
- Performing multi-step operations involving numbers
- Using a calculator
- Meanings of foreign phrases
- Estimating quantities
- Measuring
- Identifying colors
- Identifying shapes
- Telling time

Generic skills and

competencies

Even though often suggested by the constituency and a number of educational reformers, I've urged caution in representing content by sets and topics such as problem-solving, critical thinking, common sense, decision making, communication, learning-to-learn and the like. That is, some suggest in addition to, or sometimes instead of, teaching from a traditional subject-matter base, teach students skills that are generic in nature and trust they can be applied to a variety of specific needs in the future.

For example, a course in "critical thinking" might include instruction on such seemingly worthy behaviors as distinguishing claims from fact; developing valid arguments; assessing validity; reasoning from the general to the particular; reasoning from the particular to the general; spotting fallacies; recognizing ambiguity and many others.

The generic skill often called "problem solving" might include sub-sets such as recognizing symptoms of a problem; problem definition; root-cause analysis; decision making among alternative solutions and so forth.

On the surface of the matter, it seems like a terrific idea to teach a relatively finite set of skills and knowledge that could be universally applied to an infinite set of specific situations. If this would work, then the large amount of possible content indicated by subject-matter-based education could be drastically reduced and also increase the effectiveness of formal education. It is further suggested by some proponents of generic skills/competency education that it would solve the problem presented by my accomplishment-based approach which is we cannot anticipate all the situations the student will face post-instruction.

Teaching students to think critically, teaching problem solving, and getting them to learn how to learn, also seems to mollify somewhat the oft-raised objection to teaching specific behavioral processes "you want to make people into robots."

It would be a terrific idea except for one thing: *It simply does not work to a significant degree.* Though the matter is far from being completely settled, teaching of generic skills such as problem solving does not work very well if one defines "work" as a high degree of TRANSFER to specific situations in the FUTURE.

Review of studies on critical thinking, for example, shows some positive effects on transfer, but the gains are relatively minor and are probably not worth the time and cost.

E.D. Hirsch, Jr. in *The Schools We Need* seems to concur:

> *Instruction in critical thinking has been going on in several countries for over a 100 years. Yet researchers found that students from nations as varied as Israel, Germany, Austria, the Philippines, and the United States, including those who have been taught critical thinking, continue to fall into logical fallacies.*

And

> *People who have just finished a one-semester course in logic are only marginally more logical than people who have never taken logic. Other experiments show that training in abstract "higher-order skills" does not improve thinking.*

Let me pose a thought-experiment to test transfer. Suppose we developed three versions of a course for sales managers, and divided 100 sales managers into three matched groups. Each group completed one of the courses:

1. Problem Solving
2. Problem Solving for Managers
3. Problem Solving for Sales Managers

Immediately on completion of the course, we gave each of the groups a final exam to determine if the instruction had taught them the particular content of the course they took. Suppose each graduate scored 100% on the test.

If we then followed up each of the three groups of sales managers to see the degree they solved actual sales management problems, which group, if any, would probably perform better in solving sales management problems?

The data on transfer show that #3 would likely produce significantly greater results than #1. In fact, I'd predict a ranking in inverse to the order shown above. And, Group 1 would probably fair only a little better, if at all, than sales managers who had received no instruction at all.

Suppose we gave three matched groups of high school seniors one of these courses:
1. Principles of Communication
2. Principles of Written Communication
3. Business Letter Writing

Which group would write a better business letter? I'm afraid the more general the content, the less the transfer to specific situations; the more specific, the greater the probability of transfer.

I am NOT saying that in any given course principles, theory, whys and so forth should not be taught. I AM saying such should be taught in context with the specific behavioral process to be acquired.

In a similar vein, there is the belief in many quarters that learning knowledge and skills in one domain will transfer to a different domain. For example, learning calculus would also teach the student to "think more critically" in general. I've heard that learning Latin grammar will help the learning of English grammar. (Vocabulary, perhaps, but not grammar. In fact, I could argue that one hinders the other!) It might be said because performing a medical diagnosis requires "higher order thinking skills," then physicians will generalize the figuring-out of other things that require deep analysis and thought.

E.D. Hirsch, Jr. in *The Schools We Need* says:

> ...*an ability to think critically about chess does not translate into an ability to think critically about sailing.*

To test such belief about this kind of transfer, suppose we gave a group of medical students a course in problem solving and gave a group of computer repair technicians students the *same* course. It would be absurd to believe that the computer technicians would become better at medical diagnosis, and the medical student could then troubleshoot computers better, even though at some level of generality medical diagnosis and trouble-shooting involve problem solving.

This kind of failure (transfer to other domains) is obvious. However, as in the examples above, I suggest the data show that generic course in problem solving would not help the medical students to diagnose much better, nor would it facilitate the technicians in their quest to trouble-shoot.

It is a bitter pill to swallow, but teaching history well might result in the learning of history (if taught well and/or the students "study hard"), but as far as learning *from* history, the news about transfer is bleak. It is commonly said that a prime purpose of teaching history is so we will not repeat the mistakes of the past, and that we will repeat the successes. If this were true, then I'd propose that all our political leaders be required to have doctorates in history. (Those who have doctorates in history might allow as how this would be a fine idea.)

From many years of research and application in the field of learning I'm convinced: **The specific transfers specifically; the general not at all.** Since most formal schooling, even that which purports to teach thinking and problem solving skills, presents generalities, we should not be too surprised at the poor record of transfer.

Howard Gardner in *The Unschooled Mind* is more blunt:

> *This state of affairs [regarding transfer failure] has seldom been acknowledged publicly, but even successful students sense that their apparent knowledge is fragile at best. Perhaps this uneasiness contributes to the feeling that they or even our entire educational system are in some sense fraudulent.*

Upon graduating from college with excellent grades in electrical engineering, my son seemed to support Gardner's suspicion: *I don't know how to be an engineer. I feel like a fraud.*

Why is it that transfer of generic skills and competencies are disappointing at best, non-existent at worse? I believe it is for the same reasons as the previously discussed poor record of transfer of subject-matter-based content:

- Some students cannot see the relevancy, so attention to and learning of the content is diminished.
- Humans have difficulty generalizing from instruction to the post-instruction situation because signals and actions learned are not a close enough match.
- Information is forgotten because of lack sufficient initial fluency and lack of spaced, frequent exercise.

What we get out of all this is a probable best-to-worst hierarchy content of education—if we accept that the prime measure of "goodness" is the degree of transfer:

BEST: *Specific* **content derived directly from expected post-school accomplishments and behavioral processes**

SECOND: **Content organized by generic skills and/or competencies**

WORST: **Content organized by subject-matter categories**

10. Should School Deal with Attitudes and Values?

Any school of integrity, public or private,

secular or religious should try to help its students

become decent people

—Theodore R. Sizer
Horace's Compromise

One of the more controversial issues in educational reform centers around content of the curriculum usually called *values education*. And, by way of association, the matter of student *attitudes* becomes an issue that cannot be separated from the values students hold.

There is some organized resistance from some segments of the constituency concerning the treatment of values by the school. I interpret the resistance to be based on the belief such content should not be in the domain of public education, but is a matter reserved for the family and religious institutions.

Such a stance is supported to some degree by the *Constitution* and rulings by the courts in matters regarding separation of church and state, direct instruction favoring a particular religion over another, and school prayer. Also, in surveys taken by the Carnegie Foundation for the Advancement of Teaching in 1994 70% of the parents polled said it is the family who should carry the primary responsibility for instilling values; 29% said such should be shared by the family and the schools. Only 1% said it is mostly the school's responsibility.

My surveys of the constituency (particularly parents and employers) do not show such a clear discrimination. In fact, many of the items reported in the last chapter concerning the content desired could be termed values and attitudes rather than strictly knowledge and skills. The constituency frequently mentions *ethics, honesty, respect, responsibility, tolerance* and the like as being desired characteristics of the student as a result of public education. This also indicates to me the stakeholders believe there is a problem in these matters.

A good deal of research seems to support the view that there is a problem with values and attitudes among students. For example, in 1996 the Josephson Institute for Ethics reported the results of a survey of 11,000 high school and college students:

- 37% of high schoolers said they stole from a store in the past 12 months.
- 65% cheated on an exam.
- 24% of college students said they'd lie to get a job. In another study involving 20,000 high schoolers, two-thirds said they had cheated on a test in the last year. Nearly 90% said they'd copied another's homework.

There is no doubt we are experiencing societal problems with the young in the '90s relevant to values and attitudes. A previous chapter illuminated some of these:

- One in three young women become pregnant in their teen years, the majority are unmarried.
- 33% of high school students admitted to having used illegal drugs.
- Of the high school dropouts, more than half will appear before a judge within five years.
- 20% admitted having brought a weapon to school.

All this is not to say the schools cause these things. The causes are complex and have their roots in society. The issue relevant to this book is: Should public education try to minimize the effects of these problems by dealing directly with values and attitudes of the young?

In another, better world the answer would be no. In my opinion it should be the primary responsibility of the family, and perhaps religious institutions, to instill the positive values and attitudes in the young. The school would then support and reinforce such. However, this is not now "another, better world." Since I am a stakeholder, I want the schools to play a major role in this arena. Whether the schools should do so begins with how we, the stakeholders, define purpose of education.

I have tried to emphasize the importance of first agreeing on purpose for all things. Purpose tends to influence goals. Goals give us direction on the relevant processes. The matter of purpose is of particular importance to the issue of the school's relationship to student attitudes and values.

If we decide the school's purpose is confined to subject-matter-based academics, then it is somewhat clearer school should not concern itself with student values and attitudes. If, however, we adopt the bigger purpose offered by this book, then our attention is more directed to the possibility of these domains being targeted in addition to knowledge and skills. That is, the purpose, *to produce graduates who have S/K/I to become accomplished citizens*, might imply the model citizen has certain values and certain attitudes which are characteristic of the adjective *accomplished*.

What are values and attitudes?

Such terms as *right, wrong, honesty, ethics, tolerance, character* are abstractions. It is difficult to deal precisely with abstractions. In education there has been entirely too much abstraction and too little concreteness in knowledge and skills. The same is true with the abstractions of values and attitudes. Given adoption of my proposed purpose, we would seek to derive the specific knowledge and skills that will make up the curriculum. If the constituency so decides, we would also seek to define attitudes and values in more concrete terms.

I call such words as *respect* and *ethics* "soft terms." I define *soft* as "open to wide interpretation." For example, if we were to ask 1,000 people what is meant *beauty*, we would confirm beauty is indeed in the eye-of-the-beholder. We'd get a wide variety of definitions. If we asked 1,000 people what is meant by *vehicle*, we'd get a relatively narrow range of responses. In other words, some words are "harder" than others. This means there has been some significant AGREEMENT on meaning. *Several* is softer than *three*. *Automobile* is less abstract than *vehicle*.

To some degree all words are open to interpretation. The common word *set* has several hundred definitions in my unabridged dictionary. *Value* and *attitude* themselves have a multitude of meanings listed. To reach a consensus on content in education, we must have a way of hardening (de-abstracting) soft terms, especially concerning values and attitudes. One possible way is to approach the issue is to define value/attitude abstractions behaviorally. That is, what do people DO to make us think they have a particular value/attitude? (We can't see an attitude; we only can observe behavior.)

For example, if employers tell us they want people to have *good work ethic*, we might probe them concerning what overt actions would workers exhibit which would cause the employer to conclude employees had "good work ethic." The employer might respond with BEHAVIORS such as:
- *Comes to work on time.*
- *Finishes a task on time.*
- *Does not take unexcused absences*
- *Looks for additional work to do when finished a task.*

By defining the soft statement *good work ethic* in terms of overt behavior, we have made it less abstract. If so, we are in a much

The Eden Conspiracy

better position to obtain common agreement among stakeholders if such behaviors should or should not be part of the content of the curriculum. The schools would be in a much better position to design tactics (instructional and motivational) to influence the desired behavior. The students would be in a better position to detect the difference between when they have good work ethic and when they don't—perhaps the most important of the reasons for concreteness.

This reminds me of the time our four year-old son was going to a friend's house. As usual, my wife admonished *Be a good boy.* With all sincerity he asked, *Mom, what IS a good boy?* I don't recall what she then told him, but the question became our family's response when any of us became too soft in our speech.

We cannot observe directly attitudes and values. We can only see overt behavior. In a previous chapter I characterized behavior as either being predominately overt or covert. That is, overt actions are ones we can experience through our senses. Covert actions take place "inside" the human. *Doing* is usually associated with overt behavior. *Thinking* is a COvert behavior that is *cognitive* (knowing) in character.

I think we'd all agree there are such things as feelings that are not exactly the same as cognitive events. For example, I can *distinguish between* an orange and a lemon—largely a cognitive event. I *like* oranges—a feeling event. (In psychology, the jargon word for feelings is *affect.*)

When we speak of attitudes and values, we are usually talking about AFFECT—a person's feelings. The remark *she KNOWS the multiplication tables* is a commentary on probable cognitive behavior. The remark *he HATES math* is a comment on probable affective behavior.

Schematically, we could represent the relationship like this:

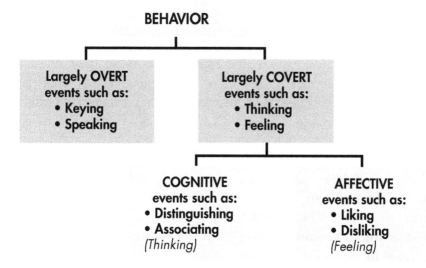

We can't directly observe covert behavior. We *infer* probable covert behavior from someone's overt actions or the output produced. For example, if I see someone stopping at a red light (overt behavior), I might infer she can distinguish between red and green signals, and can associate the correct meanings (cognitive behavior). I cannot tell her affect (feelings) about traffic lights from this one observation. In fact, it isn't any of my business.

If affect is covert behavior, we must infer its presence from overt events or the results produced, and we usually need more than one observation to do so. For example, if you observe me going to the movies twice a week, see me opting for a TV movie over a ball game, see me renting movies often, and I bore you to death with my talk about movies, you'd perhaps infer my feeling concerning movies was positive. That is, you might say *Harless probably values movies*. Or, *Harless probably has a positive attitude about movies*. Or, *Harless is probably motivated to go to movies*. (I say "probably" because one can never be 100% sure of inferences. The best we can do is talk about probabilities. It could be I really hate movies, but go because my occupation is movie critic.)

The Eden Conspiracy

So
what?

The discriminations above are important because they give us a method to deal in a more concrete and effective way with the abstract issue of values and attitudes as they relate to possible treatment in education. (Also, with motivation, as will be discussed later.)

The stakeholders cannot agree on IF the schools should deal with values and attitudes at all unless there is an agreement on what they are. The stakeholders cannot address which values and attitudes should be influenced by education unless they are defined in more concrete terms.

Teachers cannot deal with attitudes and values unless they know when they probably exist. Also, the methodologies for influencing cognitive behaviors and affective behaviors are very different from each other.

There are certain *instructional* tactics that are effective for teaching knowledge and skills. (I call this *Instructional Science* even though such designation smacks of a subject-matter organization.) There are certain motivational-like tactics teachers and parents can use to deal with student affect. We will deal with both in subsequent chapters.

I don't believe the opposition to treating values in public education stems from a belief that values and attitudes should not be dealt with at all. I think the opposition comes from certain values that have been proposed. Usually these objected-to values involve sex education, religion, politics, and lifestyle. I believe there are some values all could agree on with little difficulty such as *honesty, respect, love-of-learning, patriotism* and others, IF we take the trouble to define such abstractions in behavioral terms. The others must be and should be debated and arbitrated at the community level.

NOTE: For additional reading concerning learner attitudes and motivation, I highly recommend Robert F. Mager's delightful book *How to Turn Learners On Without Turning Them Off* published by Center for Effective Performance, Atlanta, Georgia.

146

11. Concerns About Accomplishment-Based Education

Abandoning subject-matter categories as the base for deriving content of the curriculum will seem radical to some. Subject-matter ...

...categories have served as the largely unquestioned framework for centuries. The subject-matter paradigm for the organization-of-knowledge is not likely to be changed quickly because many groups have a vested interest in subject-matter organization. Subject-matter organization is the model, not only for content of the curriculum, but for the educational publishing industry, standardized tests, teacher preparation and assignment, grades, proposed national standards, and the self-description 25% of us carry the rest of our lives—*I was a (psychology, math, history, biology) major.*

In addition to the natural resistance to a radical shifting of paradigms, there are many questions and concerns that arise about accomplishment-based education. This chapter addresses some of the ones I anticipate.

> **Concern: *Your premise is that the prime purpose of education is to contribute to the process of becoming accomplished citizens. If the constituency does not agree such is the prime purpose, the accomplishment-based structure will be difficult to employ.***

That is correct. That is why I stated previously the first and most important issues in educational reform are the purpose and goals of education. This is why I insist we must start educational reform by a thoughtful and careful consideration of purpose and goals. If the constituency continues to hold to the traditional purpose of teaching K/S/I derived from subject-matter categories, my model is seriously compromised; and, any subsequent adoption of interventions will continue to be disappointing.

> **Concern: *It is not the school's business to deal with content that has to do with values and attitudes.***

The school and the state now decide content for the most part. Many schools now deal with values and attitudes. I believe it should be the stakeholders who have the primary input to content. If the stakeholders decide which attitudes and values should be addressed, then the schools should promote those values and attitiudes.

As stated, I think the objection to values and attitudes has to do with WHICH values and attitudes should be addressed in school, not that values and attitudes should be ignored altogether. Which attitudes and values is a matter to be debated among the stakeholders.

Concern: *You could never get consensus on content.*

We could not get consensus if we didn't attempt it at all. Getting consensus could very well be a difficult task, but certainly worth trying because of the large potential payoff. My experience in business/industry/military education has shown me if I doggedly follow the retrogressive sequence outlined earlier (Purpose-Goals-Accomplishment-Behavioral processes-K/S/I) it is very much easier to obtain consensus than if I start by addressing the K/S/I issue first.

We already have evidence the debate would center around the value/attitudes issue in such matters as morals, sex education, diversity, equal opportunity, and perhaps issues associated with church-state division. I think consensus on most values/attitudes would not be too difficult to reach. Even without defining them much further, I believe we could agree on such things as the need for positive attitude toward learning, good work ethic, moderation, respect for authority, honesty and others—especially if we demystify the values by specifying them in behavioral terms.

My discussions with potential employers and parents concerning deriving content from a goal-driven accomplishment base is encouraging on the matter of reaching consensus on content not related to values. In fact, even when we did not attempt consensus among potential employers, we saw a surprising commonalty of what the employers want. While the results from poll of parents were more diverse, there was still a pattern of commonality among them.

Concern: *Your accomplishment-based approach has its origins in business/industry/military, not public education. You imply education is the same as training.*

The "education vs training" issue seems to be more important to others than it is to me. The issue arises in almost every graduate seminar and course I've ever given in college, and in many given to human resources development personnel. Further, many corporations have both an education and a training department. When we examine the two organizations, we usually find the education department teaches managers, the training department deals with non-managers. We usually find the education department uses a subject-matter-based approach to derive content. When they do, the content is predictably general and abstract; thus, the transfer is predictably weak; thus, we know the real worth (cost-benefit) is suspect. The challenge is to agree on the accomplishments, behavioral processes, and K/S/I of managers. We've been able to do that with our approach.

The objection might be based on the attitude that training is somehow inferior to education; and, education is noble and training is mundane.

I'm convinced it is the outputs of education that are, in the final analysis, valued by the stakeholder, not just the knowledge/skill/information. It certainly is not whether we call the process education, training, or any other label.

Training and education are often differentiated by saying education is to provide knowledge for unpredictable circumstances; training is for predictable circumstances. Whenever I hear that I'm reminded of a panel discussion I took part at a professional conference for learning theorists. The question from the audience: *What is the difference between education and training?* B.F. Skinner, a distinguished Harvard psychologist, responded:

> *I believe training is what you do when you know what you want students to do. I suppose education is what you do when you don't.*

The derivation of content from the goal-accomplishment-behavioral process sequence increases the chances a wide-range of circumstances will be covered.

A practical differentiation: Education is what we receive in school. Training is what we receive after school. That is, education is associated with K-college. Training is more associated with knowledge/skills/information provided by business/industry/military. I'm willing to let such a differentiation stand, if one insists on a discrimination of the two words.

I think we, the stakeholders, must be much more aggressive toward education. Part of that is to be more proactive in specifying what we want the students to accomplish and do as a result of education. If this is viewed as more of an imitation of current business/industry/military methodology, then so be it. In the last decade some organizations in the private sector have made great strides in producing learning and transfer. If so, why not adopt and adapt some of their methods for education? We can call it whatever makes us feel comfortable.

Concern: *It is difficult to see how science, math, foreign language, and history would be taught in an accomplishment-based approach.*

It could be difficult to see because accomplishment-based instruction is a different paradigm. This concern indicates to me one is still operating from a subject-matter base. Content is either accomplishment-based or it isn't. The expression *subject-matter-based accomplishment* is a non-sequitur. It would be like saying *water-basing oil-based paint.*

I can only repeat: In an accomplishment-based approach, we *derive* the relevant and important K/S/I. We derive WHAT science, what math, etc. that should be taught. HOW the content is taught is an issue addressed after the content is determined.

> **Concern: *You can't anticipate all the situations a student will face after formal education.***

That is correct. However, it is true no matter which model we use to define the content of education. We can't teach every student everything. So the issue becomes which approach is more valuable as the compromise to the impossible task of teaching everybody everything.

In a real sense, current subject-matter-based education is the compromise which opts for scope rather than depth. That is, teachers employing the subject-matter-based education paradigm traditionally try to achieve as much "coverage" as they can. (One colleague of mine calls this the "spray and pray" approach.) This has not worked very well. The case is fairly strong that most students exit formal education not being able to do very much. At best, a fraction have obtained "union cards," certifying some familiarity with subject-matter.

The compromise to the you-can't-teach-everybody-everything issue offered by accomplishment-based instruction is to inventory the stakeholders and to consult specialists in the behavioral processes specified. Doing this will help us discover the important and more frequent situations they are likely to encounter. If so, we can then make sure the students are equipped with the K/S/I and possibly attitudes/values to handle those situations in a more accomplished manner; and, that they will be reasonably fluent in doing so.

Concern: *All this sounds like "programming" the student. We don't want to produce unthinking robots.*

I too want students who can think for themselves. So much so that I don't want to leave it to chance. I want to teach them HOW to think about relevant and important things. Accomplishment-based education merely seeks to make apparent the covert elements ("thinking") relevant to desired accomplishments.

In regard to "how to think," what do we want them to think about? The quick answer is "everything." The answer assumes if we teach a generic process it will transfer adequately to specific situations as they arise. I've tried to make the case previously, as others have, that the teaching of the generic process of thinking does not work as well as teaching the specific thinking (covert behavior) in CONTEXT with the specific behavioral process being taught.

For instance, if we were teaching some process traditionally lumped under physics, we might teach the thoughts (the covert behavior) a physicist would go through to perform the process. Even if we were successful in teaching the specific thought process involved with the specific aspect of physics, there is no guarantee it would generalize to other, dissimilar behavioral processes; and, there is not even a very high probability of transferring to other sciences. Thus, I'm afraid there is no other effective choice than to teach thinking processes, such as the Scientific Method, in context. Or, at a minimum, teach it generically before the applications, then call the student's attention to the connection. Generalization is built by encountering example after example after example.

Because of recent cult activities, "programming" has taken on the negative connotation of aversive control and forcing people to do things against their original will. As far as "programming" the student goes, I want to program the instruction, not the student. In Instructional Science we prescribe the precise tactics and activities for teaching. In their heads students are free. Their insides are their business, not mine. Their outsides—their overt behavior—is, in part, my business. They should be free to choose what they think; it is their right. It is not their right to run red lights.

Instructional Science is certainly not powerful enough to program anyone in the sense people will do things against their will. Instructional Science is powerful enough to positively influence learning in an effective way.

Instructional Science is not to be associated with motivation except in the sense it produces learning via the use of effective and positive tactics, and because success breeds desire for more success.

Concern: *Students will not learn to be creative in the accomplishment-based scenario.*

The concern about creativity is akin to the "robot" issue: If we populate the curriculum with K/S/I derived out of accomplishments and behavioral processes, the students will not become creative. (Incidentally, the highest frequency of "creativity," according to my definition, is exhibited by children *before* formal schooling. If so, what are the implications about what happens to children's creativity in the formal schooling process?)

First off, the term is soft. When I probe the user for meaning, I only get examples, not definitions. People tell me about Rodin and Einstein and Andrew Lloyd Webber. Surely one would not suggest the creative accomplishments of these giants are because of schooling in a subject-matter-based curriculum.

When definitions are attempted, I hear even softer utterances such as "thinking outside the box" and "intuitive leaps" and "getting in touch with the inner child." What could these possibly mean? Researching the matter, I conclude there isn't a definition that is generally accepted—even among those who spend their lives studying and trying to teach/foster it. I suppose creativity is like pornography: We can't define it, but we know it when we see it.

If we could ever reach a consensus on a definition of creativity, then we might be able to define the behaviors (overt and covert) which satisfy the definition. If we could define the behaviors, then we might be able to teach the K/S/I which foster creativity. If we did so, I don't envision this would be much like current subject-matter-based instruction in terms of content or methodology.

Concern: *You stress relevance of content. Could teachers not show relevance of subject-matter-based content?*

Yes. But the relevant question is *relevant to WHAT?* Few teachers would admit any content they present is irrelevant. In fact, I believe the issue never occurs to many teachers. They present information for a variety of reasons. Some present subject-matter-based information because that is what they were taught and what they were hired to teach. (We tend to hire history majors to teach history.) Some present the content they find interesting to themselves. (History teachers probably majored in history because they like history.) Some present the content that will facilitate acquirement of future content. (Algebra is needed in order to learn calculus. Trig is used in physics. *Write a research paper now because in college you'll be doing a lot of it.*)

I think the better teachers now strive to link the content they teach to non-academic application as well as future academics. That is, the teacher says: *Here is the principle/operation. Now lets see an example of its use.* For instance, a math teacher might demonstrate how a particular operation could be applied to a situation such as showing students how to calculate batting averages of their favorite baseball team. The language teacher brings a menu written in French for the students to translate. Even the proverbial report on what-I-did-on-my-summer-vacation is a remote example, I suppose.

The linking of subject-matter to examples of real-world application is a positive compromise to true accomplishment-based education, but it is still a compromise. Subject-matter is still the context. The base is still subject-matter. We are still operating under a subject-matter paradigm, then attempting to justify it somehow by looking for possible application. (If the teacher cannot show an example of application, this is a sure sign of ir-relevancy. If the teacher can show only a remote application, this is a sign of low importance.)

We must determine the desired behavioral process, then look for the relevant subject-matter to support it. Not the other way around. The alternatives ranked in order of preference:
1. Accomplishment-based content
2. Subject-matter-based content plus illustrative application
3. Subject-matter-based content

If forced to compromise the full-blown paradigm shift to accomplishment-based education, I'd do #2 above, not #3. If so, then the applications selected must be meaningful to the student; be ones that are likely to be encountered by the student post-school; and, have at least a fair probability of frequency and importance. I see little merit in math "word problems," for example, which ask students to calculate the meeting point of trains going different speeds. This is not apt to come up too often in life. Nor is the math operation used likely to transfer to situations which do come up.

It is important to note even if we compromise with a subject-matter-plus-illustrative-application model, then the applications should still be *derived* in the manner I propose.

Concern: *Accomplishment-based education will not prepare students for college.*

This is NOT true. My proposed process is geared mainly for the K-12 segment of the student's life. At the end of that period less than half of the students currently opt for entry into the higher education system. If the stakeholders so specify, then accomplishments and behavioral processes relevant to preparation for additional education would be taught in the accomplishment-based approach.

K/S/I needed as prerequisite for further education could be produced from analysis of specific desired accomplishments derived from the students various roles—potential worker, family member, society member, and individual.

For example, three of the likely desired accomplishments in the role of potential worker are: *preliminary decision concerning career choice; preparation for seeking employment;* and *decision regarding formal schooling needed for career.* These are likely to yield behavioral processes, and therefore the K/S/I relevant to preparation for college.

Other likely accomplishments which would yield specification of K/S/I needed for further education include: *acquisition of prerequisites for life-long learning; interpretation of general reading; information from references; interpretation of social issues* and others.

We should also note many of the behavioral processes likely to come out of an analysis of desired accomplishments would facilitate success in further education. Examples: composing written messages; planning use of time; using the library; gathering information from electronic media; weighing pros and cons; speaking in public; performing math operations; listening; controlling personal finances; editing written materials; measuring quantities; performing statistical operations; speaking grammatically; distinguishing fact from opinion.

If the constituency so decides, many of the attitudes/values treated would also be relevant to the facilitation of further education. Examples: staying on-task; delaying gratification; appreciating art; dealing with frustration; appreciation of literature; adapting to change.

Incidentally, a pressing issue is not getting *into* college. There is a buyer's market at present for spaces in college. The number of colleges that are highly selective is very small compared to the total number. The number of students who seek admission to the Stanfords, Harvards, MITs is minuscule compared to the total number of college-bound students.

What we often have now is the college-prep tail wagging the curriculum dog. Many schools seem to behave as if college-entrance were the only end. Those who don't aspire to college are tracked into a general or a vocational curriculum. I sometimes get the feeling the educational system regards these students as second-class citizens. (For example, money spent for vocational education is several times less than for the college-prep path, yet the number of students who don't seek four-year colleges is greater.)

When school systems boast, it is usually about the number of their graduates who go on to college. This is especially true of most private K-12 schools who make no bones about it: The final end is college-acceptance. They do this because the parents who will pay the tuition often have the vision that getting-into-college is the goal, not preparation for accomplished citizenship.

I once addressed the faculty of a private school about ways of improving instruction. As I always do, my initial question concerned their view on the purpose and goals of education. As might be predicted, they responded that the aim at this school was college-of-their-choice acceptance for every graduate. I then asked what should be done to achieve that end. The Headmaster replied with no hint of levity: *Accept smarter students*. There were nods of agreement all over the room.

I refrained from commenting that one of my clients, a chain of private hospitals, could model after their tactic in order to reduce mortality rate: The hospitals should accept only people who weren't very sick.

Concern: *Is there room in the accomplishment-based approach for those who want to learn subject-matter-based content just because they are interested in it?*

Yes, but *in addition* to content derived from accomplishments, not instead of it. We must be cautious that instruction in subject-matter for the sole purpose of student interest and the entertainment value does not consume time and resources to the detriment of instruction on accomplishment-based content.

I think personal interests and entertainment are ample justification for the individual to seek learning. I don't believe, however, that it is sufficient justification for the schools to necessarily *instruct* on such subject-matter. It would be impossible to include everything that everyone might want to learn. Personal interests are very diverse. Formal instruction on how to find for themselves information of personal interest would take care of this adequately, be very much more cost-effective, and be much more meaningful to the student.

Concern: *If the subject-matter paradigm is so prevalent, how can you hope to replace it with the accomplishment-based model?*

It will not be easy. The paradigm-shift will not start with the educational establishment. It is too well-entrenched. It is difficult for us to call into question the merits of things we have invested in. Educators also will see immediately the large implications to themselves and to the institutions allied to education—publishing, testing, college and so forth. The shift in thinking must begin to occur in the parent and employer segments of the constituency. In fact, there is much evidence the change in thinking is already happening.

Some stakeholders see it immediately. Most potential employers grasp the idea with relative ease because they are already undergoing the shift away from a subject-matter basis for the education they develop for their current employees. Their change in thinking about public education is being helped also because they see first-hand the unreadiness of the product of the schools. In other words, they perceive a problem and are the most receptive to trying another approach. We don't change our paradigms unless they are not working for us, and we perceive a more useful alternative.

In my town, for example, the employers were so vocal about the poor entry skills/knowledge/attitudes of new hires that our Superintendent of Education and the school board are launching a program of reform. (AND, the reform effort is an acceptable approximation of the accomplishment-based model being outlined in this book.)

Parents are the next segment which will need to come around. Though almost all parents I've talked to about education seem to think there are considerable problems with education nationwide, they tend not to regard their own children's school as all that bad. Most, not being involved directly with the schools, have little evidence one way or the other.

When I present to parents some the ideas presented thus far in this book, I usually get a very favorable response. They typically agree to the broader purpose and goals I pose. Most understand the argument against subject-matter-based instruction presented in Chapter 6. They get enthusiastic when I poll them about desired accomplishments and behaviors they want their children to be able to produce and do. (They also invariably raise the concerns being addressed in this chapter.)

In sessions with all constituencies, I often ask them to play a devil's advocate game concerning content and methodology of education. Some of the many issues they have raised and discussed:

- Why devote so much time teaching how to extract square-root when it is so infrequently needed? How many of us remember how to do it? Besides, even the most inexpensive calculators have a button that does the calculation instantly?
- Why is so much time spent teaching Roman numerals? To enable kids to tell time on the few clocks that have them?
- Unless jobs in the biological and medical sciences are known to be down the road for the students, why immerse the kids in endless memorization of plant parts, anatomy of the frog, genus and species names of obscure animal life? Why not teach the biology to support relevant things such as: avoiding contamination and infections; selecting healthy foods; administering first aid; making decisions concerning the environment; interpreting claims for weight-loss schemes, health products, and patent medicines; making decisions concerning procreation and caring for the young?

- Unless one is targeted toward a career in science, engineering, or architecture, how much math beyond arithmetic will 90% of the kids ever need to use? Why isn't statistics and probability taught? If math is the "handmaiden of the sciences," why isn't the relevant math taught *with* science?

- Unless we are seeking to prepare students who aspire to become historians, why not teach the events of the past relevant to interpretation of current and future issues? Is the purpose of teaching history to give students a knowledge-base so they will understand historical references when reading books and newspapers and/ or to be interesting conversationalists? If so, why not work backward from allusions in newspapers and books to such things as *Achilles' heel, the Trail of Tears, the cradle of civilization,* the *Great Society, Pandora's box* and the like?

  Is a purpose, as always intoned by history teachers, to help students avoid mistakes of the past? If so, the strategy is not working. Why not relate current events and near-term issues to precedents in history?

- Why teach Latin at all? To facilitate English? If so, why not just teach English better? Is it to enable students to decode frequently used Latin phrases such as *quid pro quo; et al; pro bono; e pluribus unum, etcetera,* etc.? If so, why not teach the frequent ones in a matter of an hour or two? Is Latin taught because so many words in science have Latin roots? If so, would it not be better to teach the vocabulary of science when teaching science?

- Why teach a foreign language at all? If it can be justified, why not teach it to fluency? Why not begin to teach it in the very early grades and continue to teach it every year? Do we really expect students to be able to converse with persons in their native tongue after a couple of high school and college courses? To be able to read a foreign newspaper, which even those with college degrees in the language often find difficult to do?

If the students will need a foreign language for their jobs later, or they simply want to learn one, there are very effective commercial programs for that purpose—and, their employers would likely pay for it, not the taxpayer.

Concern: *Accomplishment-based content will not solve all the problems of education.*

That is correct. I do not suggest it will. The paradigm shift to an accomplishment basis for deriving educational content is not a magic bullet. Though it could be one of the solutions which would minimize the effects of social problems, accomplishment-based content would not in itself eliminate all the current contributing causes of inadequate preparation of the young.

A hungry child is only somewhat more likely to concentrate on content derived from relevant desired accomplishments than she/he would on traditional content. Children presenting themselves to the formal education system with scant vocabularies, demonstrating few social skills, and the like demand interventions in addition to revision of curriculum content.

Also, revision of content will not directly eliminate poor instruction. This demands interventions I've grouped under the name *Instructional Science.* We must improve both what we teach AND how we teach AND how we deal with student motivation.

12. WHEN to Teach (Curriculum Design)

WHAT should be taught involves analysis.

Analysis means to break down into parts.

When should it be taught involves design.

The essential decisions in education are:

1. **WHAT should be taught?**
2. **WHEN should it be taught?**
3. **HOW should it be taught?**
4. **How WELL was it taught?**

WHAT should be taught involves analysis. *Analysis* means to break down into parts. WHEN should it be taught involves design. *Design* means to put together according to the findings of the analysis. HOW should it be taught involves delivery of the content to the student. How WELL was it taught involves testing and evaluation.

If our purpose was to improve our living condition, we might seek to build a new house. We'd first analyze the functions the new house must accommodate, our likes and dislikes about houses, how much money we can spend etc. We'd then develop a series of blueprints. The blueprint is the output of the design process. The builders would use proven techniques to guide them to construct the house. We'd then evaluate the house.

When we breakdown the goals of education into desired accomplishments, behavioral processes, and K/S/I, we are engaging in an analytical act. Analysis is not very valuable if we stop there, but it is an absolutely essential requirement.

Medical diagnosis *(analysis)* is not valuable unless the physician then prescribes treatment. The treatment designed is no good unless the medical staff delivers the treatment well. The accomplished physician runs tests to determine if the treatment worked *(evaluation)*.

In order to improve education, not only must the content be derived from an accomplishment base *(analysis)*, but the methodologies of Instructional Science should be employed to decide WHEN to teach *(design)* and HOW to teach *(delivery)*; and, the learning should be evaluated to see if the design and delivery were effective.

One of the aims of education should be: to produce learning of relevant K/S/I by all students. I believe this aim is furthered when we follow a systematic, engineered approach to instruction. Any systematic, engineered approach involves the same four elements. The approach involves these overall phases which are compatible with the overall issues of education:

1. ANALYSIS: Specify content.
                   (*WHAT* to teach.)

2. DESIGN: Plan components of the curriculum.
                   (*WHEN* to teach.)

3. DELIVERY: Produce learning.
                   (*HOW* to teach.)

4. EVALUATION: Produce data on acquisition.
                   (*How WELL* content was learned.)

Given the analysis, we are ready to design.

A general model for curriculum design

Given the content from the analysis phase, it is then possible to specify WHEN the K/S/I will be acquired. To do that, we first need a model that would be useful as a guideline. I see no reason why we should not use the current names for the instructional components: *Course, Module, Unit,* and *Lesson.* The relationship would look like this:

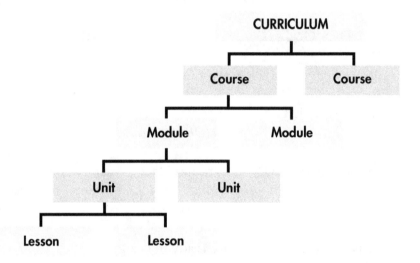

Thus, a course is two or more modules, a module is two or more units, and a unit is two or more lessons.

The model for breakdown of content previously described is: *goal, major accomplishments, behavioral processes,* and *specific K/S/I.*

The two hierarchies could be integrated roughly:
Curriculum = Goal
Course = Major Accomplishment
Module = Behavioral process
Unit and Lessons = Specific K/S/I

For example, if we were designing a curriculum in business for the job of *Salesperson,* a partial general configuration might look like this:

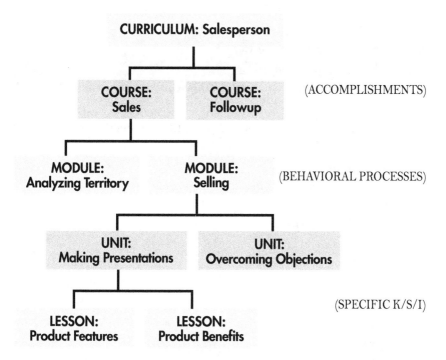

Suppose we were developing a curriculum for the job of *Clinic Nurse.* Note the courses in the curriculum would correspond roughly with the major accomplishments:

Curriculum: *Clinic Nurse*
Courses:
- *Clinic Setup*
- *Mass Inoculations*
- *Physician Assistance*
- *Emergency Treatments*
- *Patient Care*

Example modules (roughly compatible with the behavioral processes):

Course: *Mass Inoculations*
Modules:
- *Recruiting patients*
- *Taking patient history*
- *Giving injections with jet-injector*

The units and lessons would present the specific K/S/I:

Example units:
Module: *Giving injections with jet-injector*
Units:
- *Prepare patient*
- *Operate injector*
- *Maintain injector*

Example lessons:
Unit: *Operate injector*
Lessons:
- *Names of parts*
- *Cautions*
- *Calculating the dosage*
- *Operating the delivery mechanism*
- *Inspecting the injection*

The same model works as the basis for the design of public education. Although the names of the curriculum components would remain the same, the content of the increments might be very much different from the traditional subject-matter-based curriculum.

I propose *four* curricula corresponding to the four roles of the student: *Individual Life; Work Preparation; Society Life; Family Life.*

For example, a partial general design for two of the curricula might be:

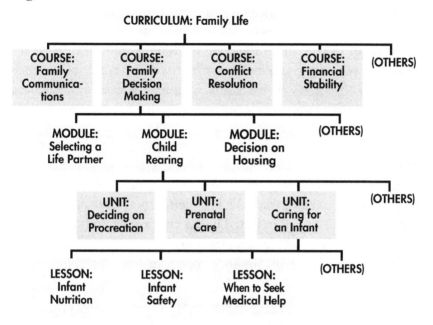

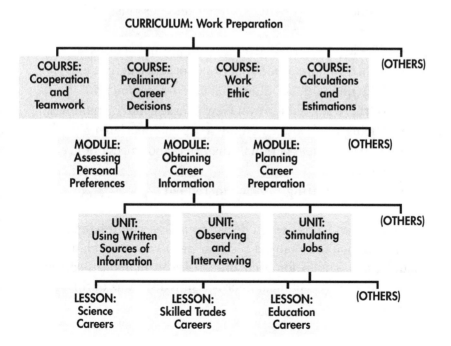

Given the hierarchies such as the above, we would then examine the Units and Lessons to determine the PREREQUISITE knowledge, skills, and information needing to be taught to enable the student to learn the content. These would become the true BASIC K/S/I to be taught. And, in all likelihood, would be taught in the early years of schooling and/or in context with increments outlined. Examples of likely basic skills: reading, vocabulary, spelling, counting, estimating, oral expression, listening, keyboarding, cause-effect recognition.

Given the content and the hierarchies, we would then make a series of macro-design decisions. The details of these design decisions go much beyond the big picture purposes of this book, but involve fairly sophisticated issues that are part of Instruction Science. Examples of design decisions:

- The sequence of the increments to teach prerequisite K/S/I
- When to begin instruction in each curriculum
- Sequence of courses within the curricula
- Sequence of modules, units, and lessons within the courses
- The levels of reality of the signals and actions
- When to have student perform practice activities
- When to conduct interim and end-assessments
- If there is need for overview courses and/or modules
- Pacing method for each instructional increment
- Type of instructional material and media for each increment
- Physical setting for each increment

The example macro-design decisions above would be manifest as overall curriculum plans, a plan for each course, a plan for each module, and a plan for each unit. (Lesson plans are contingent on certain highly technical micro-design decisions outlined in the next chapter.)

If we follow the progression being outlined, the student's day might look very much different than it does now. For example, this might be a day in the early school life of the children of Eden:

Instructional Event:	Learning Activity:
Treasure Hunt	Find words in school signs and newspaper headlines
I Write Right	Key and handwrite words found
Off-to-Work-We-Go	Discussion of relatives' jobs and the things they might need to know to do them
Feeling Good	Psychomotor skills game and exercises
Safety First!	Finding unsafe conditions at school, home, and streets
Lunch Munch Bunch	Discussion at lunch about nutrition
We Are Number One!	Computer-based arithmetic supermarket game
What Does It Mean?	Summarize main idea from story
I Wish I Knew	Finding information in the library
All Together Now	Review of things learned today and importance to their lives
Mom, Let Me Show You How to ...	Practice K/S/I at home

A day in the life of an older student might look like this:

Instructional Event:	Learning Activity:
Career Preparation	Simulating the work of a chemist
Social Issues Decisions	Researching and discussion of present effects of the organized labor movement
Family Participation	Communicating with parents
Intellectual Development	Summarizing main points of essays
Financial Decision Making	Calculating finance options
Personal Development	Discriminating artists and their works
Personal Interests	Soccer team practice

I have a strong bias that the more precise the design of anything, the better. It is unthinkable we'd surrender to chance the building of airplanes without a precise design. We would not trust our hard-earned money to a bank that had no system for accounting for the funds or no methodology for deciding loan-granting. We would not choose to live near a randomly designed nuclear power plant.

Why then would we tolerate schooling that is often poorly designed and sometimes chaotic? (A bigger question is why would we tolerate an often chaotic society, but that will be the subject of future commentaries.)

Somehow the idea of precision in the design and delivery of instruction either has not been considered, or the very idea of precision in instructional design and delivery is an anathema to some educators. Precision in educational design is often thought to be in opposition to "academic freedom." It is thought by some to constrain the teacher's "creativity."

In general, most schools give at least lip-service to design. Teachers are required to submit lesson plans in most places. Teachers report to school a week or two before the start of the year for planning. What is deficit, I believe, is that all of the designs from the entire curriculum all the way down to the daily lesson plans are subject-matter-based. Second, the designs usually only designate the sequence in which the content will be "covered." Third, in traditional instructional design there is no specification of the precise instructional tactics that will be employed to deliver the instruction.

If we analyze from an accomplishment base, the first deficit (subject-matter base) will be minimized. The second and third deficits (absence of precise design of curriculum, courses, units, and lessons, and absence of precise teaching tactics) can only be solved if teachers are provided with the knowledge and skills of what I've called *Instructional Science.*

My approach to Instructional Science contains guidelines on HOW to teach.

13. How to Teach

I hear and I forget.

I see and I remember.

I do and I understand.

—Chinese saying

I am fully aware *Instructional Science* implies a subject-matter-like grouping of what is known about influencing learning via instruction. I risk being accused of not practicing what I preach; but it is efficient to talk about influencing the acquisition of K/S/I under that designation.

Perhaps instructional *engineering* would be a more appropriate name because we emphasize *application*, not just theory, principles and facts. Nevertheless, we have derived the design and delivery procedures of instruction out of experience that is research-based, rather than artistic or anecdotal.

Although there are some "if's" and "but's" and exceptions, the overall guiding tenets of Instructional Science are:

1. **All students can learn; the majority can learn to a high level.**

It is commonly held by many of the educators with whom I've dealt, and perhaps the public at large, that the level of learning a given student can achieve is somehow fixed before students present themselves for schooling. Thus, success or failure in learning is due largely to predetermined characteristics such as "intelligence," "drives," "innate ability," and the like. An indicator to me of this strongly held belief are verbal labels given to the student such as:

- *He isn't college material.*
- *She is an under/overachiever.*
- *He isn't working up to his potential.*
- *She is a C student.*
- *My class this year is below average.*

One might accuse me of over-reaction, but to me the labels above are the philosophical kin to statements such as:

- *Girls aren't wired to do well in math.*
- *Asian Americans are good with computers.*
- *African Americans have low capacity for language.*
- *White boys can't jump.*

The belief in fixed-potentials and fixed-deficits can have devastating effects on learning and accomplishment. Labels such as these tend to become self-fulfilling prophecies. The beliefs get converted to expectations by the teacher and by the students themselves. A good deal of research into the matter seems to show **one of the stronger influences on achievement is expectation.** All too often IQ test scores, past history of poor school performance, the socio-economic status of the student's family, the student's racial/ethnic background, and even gender influence the school's expectations. These expectations often influence the effort put forth by teachers, especially for those students regarded to be "low level."

Raising expectations alone can have a very positive effect on student behavior and accomplishment. However, if we marry high expectations to good teaching methods and to appropriate motivational techniques, we can have a reasonable probability to obtain high student performance, no matter who presents themselves to the schools for instruction. We cannot guarantee high levels for every student, but we can certainly engineer it so there is considerable improvement.

I have found most teachers are genuinely concerned about student learning. (We, like Eden, should not tolerate otherwise.) But I also find almost all teachers with whom I've worked are ignorant of the precise techniques to influence HIGH levels of learning and motivation in the large majority of students, no matter the characteristics of the student. Teachers might have been "exposed" to some of the generalities in their educational methods and educational psychology courses, but as with any content that is not specific, the transfer is relatively low.

There is case after case in the literature where previously low achievers have been carried to high levels of learning via the use of precise instructional and motivational techniques. Still, the fixed-potential/fixed-deficit belief persists among many educators and the public.

James Escalante, whose efforts were dramatized in the movie *Stand And Deliver*, threw off the stereotypical labels about Los Angeles barrio children, and taught them calculus to a high level of learning.

Marva Collins peopled her private school with ghetto children who had failed in Chicago public schools (failed by the schools?), and apparently taught them to achieve to levels that surprised everyone—except Ms. Collins. (If interested in the relationship between expectations and achievement, I suggest reading *Marva Collins' Way* by Marva Collins and Civia Tamarkin.)

John McKee and his colleagues at Draper Correctional Center, a prison for young adult offenders in Alabama, used some of the techniques and materials of Instructional Science to improve dramatically the learning in "hopeless" young men, many of whom were functionally illiterate at the start of the Instructional Science intervention.

The Morningside Academy in Seattle, a private school for youths with learning problems, report student gains an average of almost three grade levels per year. In fact, they guarantee return of tuition if the student does not gain at least two grade levels in a year, as measured by national standardized tests. Morningside employs a rigorous application of instructional techniques drawn from Instructional Science.

The Precision Teaching Project in Great Falls, Montana, using the methods of psychologist Ogden Lindsley, showed that only 20 to 30 minutes per day of instruction, using a rigorous application of instructional and measurement techniques, improved elementary school students' basic skills achievement test scores by averages of 20 to 40 percentile points, depending on the skill area measured.

Carl Binder has demonstrated in a number of projects the effectiveness of achieving fluency (speed and accuracy) using precise instructional and practice techniques.

My organization's standard for achievement in Instructional Science, when applied to business/industry/military education, is "90/90." That is, at the end of the instruction at least 90% of the students will score 90% or above on criterion tests. Analogous to public education, this means almost all the students would earn A's.

My organization has designed projects on a couple of occasions where 100/100 was the only acceptable level. That is, only perfect post-instruction performance would be tolerated. (Would you want fly with a pilot whose performance was 90%? Live near a nuclear plant where the operators could not diagnose 10% of the potentially hazardous problems?)

Admittedly, the students in the business/industry/military situation have been pre-selected and are usually already motivated to learn, but the disparity between these results and the achievement distribution in traditional public education has to cause us to examine the differences in instructional techniques in addition to individual differences in the entry "goodness" of the students.

2. We must respond to individual differences in students.

Paul Brandwein in *Memorandum: On Renewing Schooling and Education* said: *In curriculum and instruction there is nothing so unequal as equal treatment of the unequal.*

There is little doubt there are many individual differences in students which will affect the level of learning. Children vary in the sundry types of intelligence, but IQ tests measure only one or two of the types. Some students come from home environments which do prepare them for schools that are traditionally designed. There is some evidence children could have differing "learning styles"; some of these styles do not match up with the teaching methods employed in the traditional schools. Some students come with attitudes and values which run counter to those of traditional schooling. Some children acquire K/S/I at a slower rate than others. Some are inquiring and aggressive; some are passive and meek.

There are individual differences in students, but for the most part school treats them generally the same in terms of design and delivery. The same instructional technique is used for all students. Students are given the same amount of time to master a given body of knowledge. The same teaching technique is used no matter the student. They enter the progression together at five or six years old; they exit together 12 or 13 years later. (Some leave the stream voluntarily when they legally can, or are consigned to the judicial system to remediate their deficits.)

The attempts to cope with individual differences by the traditional educational system are gross at best. There are two or three "tracks," of course: college-prep, vocational, and general. The "brighter" student is sometimes provided advanced courses or programs for the "gifted." (These are still subject-matter-based, lock-stepped, and employ conventional instructional tactics.) Occasionally, a child gets to skip a grade. Often teachers lavish individual attention on these children.

The children at the other end of the continuum are all too seldom provided remediation by the school. The concerned teachers work with the "slow" student as much as they can in an already over-burdened day. Some students are required to repeat a grade, where they are given the same content and treatment again in hope it will "take" this time. There is a rising recognition of so-called learning disabilities and some attempt by some schools to respond.

Children have individual differences. Using a medical analogy again, so does each patient who presents herself/himself to the physician. Good physicians do not abandon the patients who are much sicker than the majority coming for treatment. In fact, the good physician expends heroic efforts for these. Good physicians do not treat all patients alike, but respond to their individual differences.

The good architect does not design the same house for all of us. An architect treats our individual differences in the functions that will occur in our house, our particular financial situation, the variation in style preference and so forth.

Children have individual differences. If a given difference presents a barrier to learning, teachers cannot eliminate the root-cause. The teacher was not there to talk and read to the child in the early years. The teacher cannot go back and eliminate impoverished home environments. To whatever degree genetics play a role in learning and learning styles, the schools cannot change predisposition. I submit, however, schools can do things that tend to minimize the effects.

In Instructional Science we have tried to determine which differences seem to matter the most, and prescribe strategies and tactics to minimize the effects of some of the differences.

Of the individual differences in students, we believe that learning TIME is one of the more important ones. That is, if we first take the stance all students can learn, and the majority can learn to high levels, then an important variable is how long the student is given to acquire the K/S/I prescribed. The ideal is: As long it takes. This would be ideal, but, as a practical matter, it is not probable this can be done.

If it is probably impractical to give unlimited time for learning for every student, we can certainly lengthen the time for some students and shorten the time for others. This means we allow INDIVIDUAL PACING to some degree. If the teacher had only one student, then individual pacing would be a simple matter, but it is obviously not practical to provide a one-to-one student-teacher ratio in the conventional sense.

Individual pacing is possible and practical in an unconventional sense. There is a growing availability of instructional programs which allow for individual pacing. Self-instructional, paper-based material is suitable for many types of content. The computer and other types of high-tech media are useful for other types of content. Teachers can be taught how to prepare assignments which allow for in-school and at-home study that are individually paced. Tutoring and individual help are forms of individual-pacing.

It is theoretically possible that much of the entire K-12 curriculum could be individually paced, but I am not necessarily advocating such. I am merely pointing out the importance of responding to differential learning rates of students.

I want to also issue a word of caution: Although use of computer-delivered instructional programs is one of the strategies that can help in the aim of Instructional Science to move to more individualized instruction, we must not believe it is the *hardware* of instruction that is the important thing in improving instruction. We can prepare a poor instructional program and deliver it on high quality machinery. That has been done in many cases. Like teachers, preparers of instructional programs are often ignorant of what really makes the difference between quality instruction and low quality. It is instructional techniques and tactics, not the medium, that are the major influences on learning. And that is the next tenet of Instructional Science…

3. Good instruction is the major influence on learning. Thus, we improve learning by improving instruction.

Just as there are many individual differences in students, there are many influences on learning, for example: the student's history of success/failure in learning; amount of stimulation received prior to school; match of learning style and teaching style; cultural background; economic aspects of the family; nutrition; instructional tactics employed; student interests; meaningfulness of the content; physical design of classrooms; parental involvement in the learning process; attitude of peers regarding school.

Teachers cannot deal with all the influences on learning. For example, teachers can do little directly with the some of the aspects of the characteristics of students. The correction of a poor learning environment is often a larger matter than is under the control of the individual teacher. Teachers can only deal with effects.

I find it useful to categorize the influences on learning in four, sometimes overlapping and interacting categories:

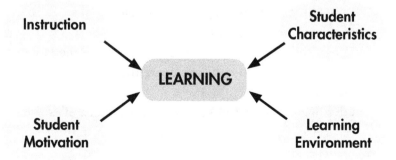

Instructional Science does not denigrate the importance of the other categories, but deals more directly with the *instructional* influences.

At present, the state of Instructional Science is "probabilistic." That is, it is not at present a hard science like physics or chemistry where there are laws and absolute values such as the Law of Gravity, the speed of light, the atomic weight of elements. Instructional Science is more akin in character to emerging sciences such as psychology, where there are little or no known laws, but are composed of rules-of-thumb, which is another way of saying *probability*.

For example, in psychology there is a principle: *A positive consequence increases the probability of recurrence of the action*. In economics there are probabilistic rules such as *when supply increases, demand tends to decrease*. Note the terms *tends to* and *increases probability of* instead of *will*.

Although Instructional Science is probalistic, we still have a large body of quite specific, data-supported tactics for instruction. This comes as a surprise to many.

A few of the scores of specific rules and guidelines regarding HOW to teach in my particular model:
- When teaching discrimination of signals, present no more than four in one instructional lesson.
- When teaching a rule, present the rule, then a narrow range of examples, then non-examples of the rule, then a wider range of examples.
- When teaching a sequence of actions, give the student a verbal organization before presenting the sequence of steps.
- Give feedback to the student immediately. If student response is correct, give confirmation feedback. If incorrect, give process feedback.

- If the students have beliefs which contradict the rule being taught, use the induction tactic.
- Sub-group signals for presentation to the student by similarity of signal. Present the most difficult sub-group first.
- If there is great disparity between signals and actions, provide a mnemonic.
- After full presentation of the concept/procedure, provide an opportunity for student response with prompts. After a cued response by the student, provide opportunity to respond without cues.
- For very difficult discriminations, present simplified versions of the signals first, then call for gradual increasingly realistic discriminations.
- When teaching psychomotor sequences, teach the students to say the steps first, then demonstrate the steps at full speed, then teach the steps in small instructional increments

Many teachers might have been exposed to some of the general aspects of Instructional Science in their education courses in college. In the main, however, the content of most teacher-training curricula is imprecise and general. Generality and imprecision result in poor transfer.

I was chagrined in the few educational courses I took as a student, such as Educational Psychology and Educational Methods, that they rarely employed the very principles and methods they espoused. For example, I once took a course that included how to use media in the instruction. The professor lectured the entire semester without using any medium other than his voice!

As incredible as it might sound, there are a few studies which seem to show that persons who had not taken education courses obtained results as good as those teachers who were certified and experienced teachers. There are also studies which lead one to believe a student's peer could be equally or more effective than the classroom teacher.

The gap is large between the findings from learning research and what gets established the repertory of the teacher. The United States Department of Education seemed to recognize this when it prepared a booklet in the late '80s titled *What Works: Research About Teaching and Learning.* The document boiled down some of the research into guidelines. Paraphrased examples:

- Help students develop good study skills.
- Have the students read a lot.
- Require students to do carefully prepared homework.
- Set and communicate high expectations to students.
- Explain exactly what students are expected to learn.
- Have students memorize factual information as basis for understanding and critical thought.
- Teach science by having students do experiments.
- Teach children to read using phonics.

We should laud the Department for their intent and effort. The guidelines are fine as far as they go; but compare the level of the examples from *What Works* above to my previous list gleaned from my version of Instructional Science. I doubt the teachers who read the much-touted booklet transferred the suggestions to the classroom. (If fact, I recently heard one of the authors say as much, but seemed to blame the non-transfer on teacher apathy rather than their booklet's generality.) If so, one of the major reasons is the lack of specificity provided.

The specific tends to transfer specifically, the general not at all.

I am always shocked at the distance between the research in learning and teaching and what gets applied in the classroom. Sometimes it seems to me as if there is a loose conspiracy by the educational establishment to maintain the status quo.

A big case in point adds fuel to my paranoia: In the '80s the largest federally funded educational experiment in history (nearly $1 billion), called Project Follow Through, compared the effectiveness of 22 models of teaching. One model, Direct Instruction, was a precise approach to teaching, employing many of the elements I've lumped under Instructional Science. The Direct Instruction methodology surpassed all others on all measures. Most of the models tested faired worse than even conventional approaches to teaching. The results were not communicated to front-line teachers. In fact, some of the less effective programs received more funding.

4. Improvement in learning is influenced by a carefully designed and delivered approach.

In addition to careful attention to the content of each segment of the curriculum (courses, modules, units, and lessons), my version of Instructional Science calls for a structured approach at the unit and lesson levels. Below is a simplification of my basic model for each unit of instruction:

Preview: Give the student the big picture of the K/S/I to be learned in the unit; how it fits in with K/S/I taught in other modules of the course; and, the consequences for learning the K/S/I as it relates to the accomplishment.

Presentation: Provide the content of the unit to the student in a series of lessons; in each lesson give the student the opportunity to respond to the signals with cues; give the student an opportunity to respond to the signals without cues; give feedback to the student.

Practice-to-fluency: Provide the student the signals at a higher level of reality and give opportunity to exercise all K/S/I presented in the lessons at a high rate of speed. If applicable, have the student integrate the content with previously presented content. Provide feedback as soon as practical.

For example, suppose within a sequence of basic skill courses dealing with reading we were teaching a module on recognizing parts of speech in a sentence. One unit of the module might concern lessons on recognizing verbs in written material: (Simplified for purposes of illustration.)

Lesson 1: *(Preview)* Show students written sentences with verbs highlighted. Tell students at least one verb must always be present in a complete sentence, and why they should learn to recognize them.

Lesson 2: *(Presentation)* Give students the definition of verb. Show examples of verbs not in a sentence. Show student examples of verbs mixed in with other words. Have students select the verbs. Give feedback.

Lesson 3: *(Presentation)* Give students a different list of words. Have student select the verbs, given partial definition. Require students to respond as fast as possible. Give feedback.

Lesson 4: *(Presentation)* Give students list of words without the definition of verb. Require students to select verbs as fast as they can. Give feedback.

Lesson 5: *(Practice-to-fluency)* Give students several sentences. Have students select the verbs as fast as they can. Give feedback.

Lesson 6: *(Practice-to-fluency)*: If previous unit(s) taught the recognition of other parts of speech, give students sentences and have students to name verbs AND previously presented part(s) of speech as fast as they can, Give feedback.

The simplified unit plan above contains several instructional techniques that are part of my version of Instructional Science including:

- Giving student a context for the specific content of the unit
- Presentation of content in relatively small increments
- Providing a rule (definition in this case)
- Providing signals (the words) and calling for action (the name of the parts of speech)
- Frequent active response by the student
- Frequent and immediate feedback
- Progression from low level of reality (word alone) to high level of reality (sentence)
- Integration of content
- Achievement of fluency (correctness with speed)

If the six lessons were to be given, the probability is high almost all students would achieve a high level of learning. AND, it would probably take no more than 20-30 minutes for the unit. AND, the lessons could be presented by the teacher and/or via some other medium such as overhead transparencies or a computer-based program.

5. The characteristics of the content largely determine teaching tactics, NOT the characteristics of the learner.

This is a quite technical issue and requires explanation beyond the big-picture purpose of this book, but in essence it says: *WHAT we teach helps determine HOW we should teach.*

That means, for example, certain instructional tactics are used when a sequence of steps is to be learned, as is the case for most math and statistics. A different set of tactics is employed when teaching concepts and principles. (Which is what science is largely composed.) Still a different group of techniques is applicable to influence the acquisition of psychomotor skills such as handwriting, keying, task requiring hand-eye coordination, and even some aspects of speaking. If the content to be learned involves distinguishing signals from each other and responding differentially, the research is quite specific on how to teach it. Combinations of techniques are required when the content represents various combinations of characteristics.

To develop my version of the process of applying Instructional Science, I revisited the research on teaching and learning, and worked out the match-ups between the type of content and the instructional tactics that are applicable. For example, if the content of the instructional unit involves psychomotor skills (such as keying, assembly, most sports tasks, handwriting) the research seems to show these tactics should be used:

- Teach students to *say* the steps first.
- Illustrate the skill in real-time speed.
- Break sequence down in small steps and demonstrate last steps first.
- Teach students to mentally rehearse the steps before practicing
- Have students practice as rapidly as possible.
- Require practice until desired level is reached.

The tactics employed in teaching a given psychomotor skill would be essentially the same no matter if the student came to the instruction with good manual dexterity, for example, or was a klutz in that dimension. We would employ the tactics in a different manner to treat the individual differences. For example, we'd use differential teaching step sizes and allow more time and more practice for the klutz.

I once analyzed, designed, and developed an instructional program for a medical research and education organization who wanted to improve a 40-hour course they were currently presenting. The organization wanted the course improved because the graduates were not learning to a sufficiently high level.

The K/S/I concerned the microscopic identification of an organism which causes a particular disease. The visual identification involves a complex set of very fine discriminations of structures in the nucleus and body of the organism. Learning research shows an instructional technique called *shaping* is the most effective way of handling this type of learning problem. (Shaping is a methodology that involves gradually proceeding from simplified discriminations to more realistic discriminations in small instructional steps.)

After taking the new course, the students exceeded the targeted 90/90 criterion level. AND, the course was reduced from 40 hours to about four.

It should also be noted the students represented a fairly wide range of characteristics: Some were laboratory technicians without a college degree, some were medical students, some were professionals with advanced degrees in science. There was no significant difference in the end-accomplishment among the groups of students. ALL achieved a high level of learning as a result of the employment of the proper instructional tactics, not as a result of their individual characteristics.

All this is not to say the characteristics of the learner are unimportant. I'm saying the characteristics of the content are perhaps more important to the issue of HOW to teach.

The procedures of design and delivery of instruction I've labeled as Instructional Science can go far in improving learning for all students, but I am compelled to repeat: The strategies and tactics for how-to-teach must be applied AFTER we revamp what-to-teach.

The combination of relevant content and application of Instructional Science could go far to produce an educational Eden; however, there is still the serpent of student motivation to contend with.

14. Influencing Student Motivation

We get interested in what we get good at.

—Jerome Bruner
Toward a Theory of Learning

Whether we adopt an accomplishment-based approach or continue to employ subject-matter as the base for content, I think all agree a target of education should be to influence student LEARNING. As previously stated, there are numerous specific *influences* on learning. I've grouped the influences under four general and interacting categories: **instruction; learning environment; student characteristics; and student motivation.**

If we want to improve learning, we need to improve three of these: instruction, environment, and motivation. Some student characteristics are, of course, givens. Unlike the head of the private school quoted earlier, we don't seek to improve learning by "accepting smarter students." We believe in education for all. We believe all can learn no matter their individual differences. We need to respond to individual differences in student characteristics.

If we were to ask teachers what is the most important problem to solve in education, I'd wager a majority would not comment too much about improving instruction or the learning environment. They would probably talk about student *motivation*. If we asked parents what their most important role is in the educational process, we would probably get the same answer in a large number of cases. While all are concerned about motivation, there is little common agreement on the meaning of the term; nor are many of the research-based techniques regarding motivation being taught to, and implemented by, the teacher.

There are numerous theories concerning motivation built around such things as "internal drives," "needs hierarchy," "Theory X/ Theory Y," "self-esteem," and the like. Few of these are based on extensive trials; the evidence offered is anecdotal at best. Millions of books on such theories have been sold as part of the pop-psychology market. Some motivational speakers and speakers about motivation command almost rock-star dollars.

In practice, many parents and teachers seem to believe they can motivate students by using some combination of exhortation, threats, scare tactics, bribery, and plain old-fashion nagging.

As it turns out, the most effective motivational techniques are often overlooked and sometimes resisted. In simple terms, we deal most effectively with student motivation-to-learn by taking a positive approach. This involves doing three things:

1. **Making the content MEANINGFUL**
2. **Increasing probability of student SUCCESS**
3. **Manipulating CONSEQUENCES**

We can make the content to be learned more *meaningful* via the accomplishment-based approach already described. That is, we select and emphasize the K/S/I to be learned that will be directly valuable to the students' present and future lives, and make sure the student sees the connection.

We can increase the probability of *success* in learning via use of the strategies and tactics outlined in the previous chapter. The precision approach to instruction discussed is for the primary purpose of influencing the success of the learner. From the point of view of motivation, I suppose the cliche, "nothing succeeds like success" has more than just a grain of truth. Coach Paul "Bear" Bryant, who was often characterized as a master motivator because of his success in getting his Alabama football players to play beyond what their "talents" would suggest, was once asked by psychologist Tom Gilbert what motivational tactics he used. Coach Bryant said *I don't motivate 'em at all. I TEACH them how to win. It is winning that motivates my boys.*

It is fairly clear that **competence produces confidence**, not the other way around, as is usually espoused. Soldiers who go into combat are confident do so because they have been rigorously taught relevant knowledge and skills, not because their sergeant built up their "self-esteem." The more competent I become at public speaking, the more confident I become. We build our competence through preparation and rehearsal. Surgeons don't get their well-known self-esteem because the staff in teaching hospitals gave them pep talks when they were neophytes. They gain confidence from long hours of skill development until they are fluent.

The *manipulation-of-consequences* influence on motivation requires more explanation. First, we need a working definition of motivation.

What is
motivation?

Contrast these statements from students:

Student A:	*I can do math.*
Student B:	*I think math is important.*
Student C:	*I like math.*
Student D:	*I want to learn more math.*

Student A is making a comment on knowledge/skill learned. B's statement might be an indicator of the student's values. C is expressing a possible attitude. Student D is stating a MOTIVE.

If we were to ask people to define motivation, they would talk about *desire, likes, wants,* and other words indicating *affect;* feelings, rather than cognition. Terms describing affect are almost always soft—open to wide interpretation. To deal with the abstraction we must have a way of hardening the word. A good way to do so would be to ask: *How would you know when a student is motivated?* In all probability the answer would come back describing overt *behaviors* such as:

The student would study hard.
... completes all assignments.
... does the schoolwork without being nagged.
... persists until lesson is mastered
... has few absences.
... participates in class discussions.
... takes difficult courses.

Note the responses above are in terms of overt behavior, behavior we can observe. This is consistent with the dictionary meaning of motivate: *To move.* We can perceive movement (overt behavior). We cannot perceive covert behavior. Motivation is *affect* behavior. We infer any covert behavior from more than one observation of overt behavior. Thus, we infer affect from observations.

One can observe another *approaching* something (move toward it). We can see one *avoiding* something (move away from it). One can remain *static* (not move). Thus:

Motivation: The affect we infer from observations of approach, avoidance, or static behavior by students.

Typically, when laypersons use the word motivation, they mean it in positive terms, in the sense of approach-behavior. One might say *she is a motivated student.* This means the student DOES things which cause the observer to comment positively. When we want to comment negatively, we say *UNmotivated.* This means either the student is exhibiting avoidance-behavior or is static—not moving.

Simply put, **if the teacher and parent are to deal with students' motivation, they can only deal directly with their OVERT behavior.** We deal with covert behavior that is cognitive (thinking) with an *instructional* intervention. We can influence covert behavior characterized as affective by using tactics in addition to instruction. These tactics involve *consequences.*

Consequences

The roles heredity and environment play in the overt and covert behavior of the child is very much unsettled. The old debate between "nature vs nurture" continues. My position: Even if we settled the matter once and for all (and that is not likely in the near term), it would not make much difference to what education should do anyway—IF we pledge that education must respond to individual differences in the student.

We can't change a student's biology. If a child is genetically "disadvantaged" by poor eyesight, we give the student glasses. If the child learns at a pace slower than others, we must accommodate this. If the child is unmotivated, we must do something about it. We cannot usually eliminate the root-causes, but we must seek ways to minimize the effects.

In terms of motivation, new borns probably do not have many individual differences in approach and avoidance tendencies, but by the time they encounter schooling, considerable influences on their motivation have already occurred. From their pre-school age experience some children already exhibit approach-behavior toward reading because they've been read to. Some children come to school exhibiting avoidance of authority figures because they have had punishing experiences involving authority. Some children are static toward math because they've had neither positive nor negative experience.

As with the instructional influence on learning, I suggest taking a precision approach to influencing motivation. And, like Instructional Science, the methodology for influencing motivation is probabilistic. This means there are known techniques for increasing the chances behavior will occur, but we cannot guarantee it in 100% of the cases.

The closest thing we have to a law in regard to motivation is:

The CONSEQUENCE following a behavior tends to change the probability of recurrence of the behavior.

When I bite a candy bar (behavior), the result is a taste sensation (consequence). The annoying buzzer stops (consequence) when I buckle the seat belt on my car (behavior). When I fish (behavior), I either get a bite or I don't (consequence).

Mountains of research seems to support many rules as corollaries to the above general principle. Some of them are discussed below.

For a consequence to be most effective, it should follow the behavior with little time delay, and be clearly linked to the specific behavior to be affected.

It is better to praise (consequence) a correct action (behavior) a student exhibits immediately than to wait until the next day. The longer the delay, the less the effect of the consequence. For example, feedback on a student's written report at the end of the term is less effective than feedback the next day. Also, if a teacher says: *The specific things I like about the report are...*, it is superior to the teacher saying: *This is a good report.*

If the consequence is FAVORABLE, the probability of recurrence is INCREASED.

Suppose I bite the candy bar (behavior) and the taste is pleasant (consequence). This increases the probability I'll bite that candy bar again. In a sense, then, I become "motivated" to eat a candy bar.

The baby cries (behavior), mom picks the baby up (a favorable consequence from baby's point of view). This increases the probability baby will cry again. In a sense the baby is motivated to cry.

If the student is praised for completing an assignment on time, the probability is increased the student will complete the next assignment on time.

If coming to school results in positive consequences, the probability is increased the student will come to school.

If the behavior TURNS OFF something unfavorable, the behavior is made MORE likely to recur.

When I buckle my seat belt (behavior), the unfavorable buzzer sound ceases (consequence). This increases the probability I'll buckle my seat belt again. I am thirsty (something unfavorable). I drink a glass of water (behavior). The water turns off the thirst (consequence). I am then motivated, so to speak, to drink water the next time I'm thirsty.

The baby cries. Mom picks up baby (behavior), baby stops crying (consequence from mom's point of view). This increases the probability mom will pick up baby when the baby cries again.

We put on gloves to AVOID the cold. Sunglasses REDUCE the glare. The unfavorable is "turned off."

A drug addict turns off the body's physiological craving and pain by getting a "fix." (This is what is meant by *getting the monkey OFF my back.*) The person gets addicted in the first place because of the positive effects of the drug—the "high," but the habit is maintained by turning-off the negative physiological effects with subsequent intake of the drug.

If the consequences are ABSENT or REMOVED, the probability of recurrence is DECREASED.

If the candy bar has no taste whatsoever (absence of consequence), the probability I'll bite that candy bar again (behavior) is decreased.

If I never get any payoff from a slot machine (absence of consequence), the chance I'll play it again is decreased.

If a student is never called on when she raises her hand, the student will soon stop raising her hand.

If coming to school does not result in positive consequences or does not turn off a negative situation, students will tend to go somewhere that does produce more positive consequences.

If the consequence is very UNFAVORABLE, the person will try to AVOID (escape) the punishing situation. But the probability of recurrence of the behavior long-term is VARIED and largely UNPREDICTABLE.

If the student is beaten up by a bully at school, he'll tend to avoid the bully in the future. He might also avoid school. He might get his friends to retaliate. He might bully others. It is really unpredictable.

If a student constantly fails in school and is punished for this failure, the student might increase efforts in order to turn off the unfavorable consequences, but is perhaps more likely to try to avoid school—through absences and perhaps by ultimately dropping out.

Punishment, failure, and other negative consequences might be motivating to some students on some occasions, but it is not predictable. The only thing we can predict is an increased probability of avoidance-behavior.

Providing INCREMENTAL favorable consequences for improvement in behavior is better than punishing the student for failure or withholding consequences altogether.

Much of the Instructional Science previously outlined is for the purpose of achieving high levels of learning. Speaking in loose terms, this success is motivating to the student—the consequences (correct answers, good score on test, recognition by teacher, parent, and peers) are favorable. But the instructional techniques do not always achieve 100% achievement 100% of the time.

There is a motivational technique we call *shaping* which can be very powerful in getting the student to exhibit successful behavior. In essence, the shaping technique requires providing a positive consequence for any effort that approximates desired behavior. If student does not improve on the next try, we withhold positive consequence. We then provide positive consequence for each incremental improvement until desired fluency (correctness with speed) is reached.

Once desired behavior is established, it can be maintained by INTERMITTENT positive consequences.

We can use instructional tactics and application of positive consequences to get students to be successful and motivated. Motivation needs to be maintained. This seems to be done best by then switching to a schedule of positive consequences delivered at non-fixed intervals. (Positive consequences often lose some of their power if provided every time the student engages in a behavior.)

There are several more such rules, but these serve to illustrate the possibility of a systematic and effective approach that can be taken to deal with student affect by manipulation of consequences, especially by providing positive consequences and withholding consequences.

What are positive consequences?

First off, a consequence is something that occurs *after* a behavior is performed. This is why bribery, exhortation, nagging, threats and the like are not consequences and are not reliable motivators. Such are delivered *before* the behavior occurs in hopes of somehow "spurring on" the student, I suppose.

Behavior is shaped by its consequences. The quality of a consequence is in the eye of the receiver, not the deliverer. For example, public recognition is a positive consequence to some children, but is a punishing consequence to others. Examples of easy-to-deliver consequences from a teacher or parent usually considered positive by the student:

- Feedback that acknowledges correct behavior
- Realization by student the behavior being learned is/ will be valuable
- Verbal "pats on the back"
- Attention in form of eye-contact, smile, leaning forward
- Giving assistance when needed
- Allowing student to choose an activity to engage in

> PLEASE NOTE: In the public school setting I DON'T recommend using money or food or physical contact with the student as positive consequences. Using such consequences could have possible negative legal, health, clinical, political and religious ramifications. Also, such could be impractical to deliver. They are also not necessary because there are other positive consequences which are effective and can be delivered easily by the teacher/parent.

Positive consequences are not exactly the same as "incentives." An incentive is like a carrot dangled in front of a student *before* the student acts. An incentive is like promising a positive consequence *in advance* of behavior. Most promises of long-term positive consequence are too far out in the future and require too long of a chain of actions and contingencies to be very effective for motivating current behavior by the student. Also, teachers are not in the position to fulfill their part of the contract anyway. For example:

> *It will help you live a good life, if you get a good job. You will get a good job, if you get a college degree. To get a college degree, you must first get into college. To get into college, you must get good grades in high school. To get good grades in high school, you must learn what I'm trying to teach. In order to learn this, you must study hard, and give up a lot of things you'd like to be doing.*

That is a very long chain of contingencies for many students to understand and accept in order to motivate them to burn the midnight oil learning the names of clouds or even solving quadratic equations.

A special application: *Contingency Management*

One of the positive consequences listed above is *allow student to choose an activity to engage in*. Psychologist David Premack showed if this consequence was provided to students *after* they engaged in an activity of the teacher's choice, then it increased the probability the student would engage in the behavior the teacher chose.

Applying this finding, psychologists Lloyd Homme and Donald Tosti developed a motivational system they called *Contingency Management* (CM). Homme and Tosti calls CM an application of "Grandma's Rule": *Eat your peas and then you may have some cake.* (Note the positive nature of this contract as opposed to the threat: *If you don't eat your peas, you can't have any cake.*)

For example, suppose the teacher wants the student to work 10 arithmetic problems correctly in 15 minutes. If the student did so, then the teacher would allow the student to select and engage in an activity such as listening to tape of a story of his/her choice.

Based on Homme and Tosti's work, I implemented a modified version of CM in a class of students who were definitely not on the road to becoming accomplished citizens. They had failed academically (all high school dropouts, some semi-illiterate). They had even failed at crime. These young men were in a prison for young offenders.

I prescribed specific, small-increment academic activities and criteria I wanted them to achieve. I arranged the contingency contracts activity-by-activity: When the criteria were met, they could select from a "menu" of activities *they* had constructed. Examples of their desired activities: bull-session with a member of the staff; take a nap; be alone for a few minutes; watch a TV program; listen to music; sit in my upholstered office chair and put their feet on my desk; use my electric typewriter; get a cup of coffee from the instructional staff's urn. (I had to pull this one from the menu at the "suggestion"of my fellow staff members.)

Almost all these chronically failing students earned A's in the course. (Of course they also had a "gifted" instructor.)

General guidelines for student motivation

The research-based rules described above might be converted to a set of guidelines for the teacher and parent regarding student motivation. For example:

1. **Make the content of instruction as meaningful** to the students as possible. Show them the link between the specific K/S/I being learned and the valuable behaviors and accomplishments relevant to their current and future lives. If the content is not directly meaningful to their future lives, be honest with the student. For example, some content might need to be learned in order to score well on mandated standardized tests or be required for college acceptance.

2. **Increase the probability of success and reduce probability of failure** by employing methodologies of Instructional Science. For example, respond to individual differences in learning speed; select teaching tactics appropriate for the content; provide feedback as immediate as practical; use techniques to build fluency. (Fluency seems to build confidence as well as competence.)

3. **Provide positive consequence** as soon as possible following desired behavior; connect the consequence clearly to the behavior; shape the students to fluency by providing positive consequences for approximations of desired behavior until students can exhibit the behavior with speed and accuracy.

4. **Remove positive consequence for UNdesired behavior.**
   There is a reason for all behavior. In a large number of cases
   the reason is the student has obtained a positive consequence
   for the behavior NOT desired by the teacher or parent; and, the
   misbehavior is probably being maintained by an intermittent
   schedule. For example, a student might clown around because
   it produced favorable attention from peers. Rather than
   punishing the student for inappropriate behavior (which
   might even gain the student more attention), it might be
   better to try two things: Remove the student from the source
   of the positive consequence—psychologists call this "time
   out"; and, provide a positive consequence that is *incompatible*
   with the undesired behavior. For example, praise the student
   when he/she is NOT behaving in an inappropriate manner.
   My colleague, Robert Mager, calls this *catching them in the act
   of doing something right.*

5. **NEVER ridicule a student. Avoid threats and punishment
   as much as possible.** If we use threats and punishment
   intended as motivators, we must be prepared to threaten and
   punish continually; and, we must be prepared for the varied
   and unpredictable side-effects. (Except for avoidance of the
   source of the ridicule.)

To employ the motivational techniques described above requires
most of us to make a paradigm-shift in our stance concerning
student motivation. Many regard motivation as *intrinsic*. That is,
the desire to do something is IN the student and/or withIN the
activity itself.

There is a grain of truth, of course, in both of those. Affect is
an INternal state. Some activities seem to become INtrinsically
enjoyable in themselves without obvious value. But the real issue
is how do these feelings get INto the student? It does not seem
the student was born with most of these desires. The student
has to DO/THINK something first before experiencing the

positive or negative feelings about the activity. Joy is not IN most activities to begin with.

General states of motivation such "love of learning" is a *result* of previous behaviors which have produced positive consequences, and have generalized to other behaviors. This does not automatically happen to all.

Self-esteem

A similar issue to confidence/competence is the idea of focusing teachers on building self-esteem. This is sometimes called *affective education*. The idea, as I interpret it, is the teacher should first get kids to "feel good about themselves." This, I assume, is to counteract the tendency for teachers to hold low expectations for some students, and the low motivation of the student due to early failure. The idea, it seems, is that competence would be an output of confidence.

As pointed out, the evidence is just the contrary: **Self-esteem comes from success plus the positive consequences tied to the student accomplishment.** Students feel good about themselves when they achieve; and, when accomplishment is confirmed by feedback from the teacher, parent, and/or peers.

I could be over-reacting, but I think the concentration on self-esteem, at the expense of a focus on high levels of learning, promotes the ego-centric behavior of many of our youngsters at the present. Also, the building of a *false* self-image leads to failure in the long run, the very opposite of what any of us want.

One must not misinterpret what I'm saying. I believe all children can learn and can learn to surprisingly high levels. I believe confidence and self-esteem and feeling good about one's self are all extremely important to the stated purpose of education. But I must also be clear that such is not achieved by concentrating on confidence at the expense of competence and/or by exhortation. We achieve student motivation and self-esteem only by making the content of education valuable and meaningful, PLUS promoting student success in learning via good instruction, PLUS arranging positive consequences.

Teachers and parents cannot command a student to "be motivated," nor can they bestow self-esteem. Motivation and self-esteem are *results*, not prime-movers. There is nothing wrong with teachers and parents saying *I know you can do it.* Such could serve as setting expectations. But we must help students fulfill the expectations. We should not tolerate otherwise.

15. The Road to Eden

Like the city of Eden, any community that wants

to improve the preparation of the young in a

revolutionary way must do so in a cooperative ...

...fashion; and, do so by following the progression outlined in this book. In general terms, the following accomplishments of educational reform should be produced initially and in the sequence listed:

Accomplishment 1: *Public recognition of the need*

Problem-solving cannot occur without first admitting a problem exists. If we are happy with the society we have, we will not expend the energy to improve it. If we are satisfied with the product public education is producing, educational reform is not likely to occur. Thus, someone must first recognize the need for massive reform of education and alert their community of the seriousness of the problems.

I don't believe national or federal calls for educational improvement and the suggested interventions are likely to have a great deal of effect. Washington-based programs for educational reform have not produced significant results in the past. At best, the White House, Congress and the Department of Education can have only an abstract and general effect, and perhaps provide some informational and financial assistance. Like politics, education is a local matter when it gets right down to it.

The initial stimulus could conceivably arise from a number of sources: A concerned school board, a visionary school superintendent, a forward-looking community leader, a community activist group, the elected city council, a crusading newspaper, or an unhappy body of parents who have organized to influence educational reform. However, the most vocal segment of the constituency at present is the potential employer, and would perhaps be the best source of the compelling message that revamp of schooling needs to occur.

The only downside for local employers being the clarions for reformation is the public and educators' tendency to compartmentalize education into college-prep and vocational-technical curricula. Thus, reformation precipitated by the potential employer segment of the constituency is apt to be confined to work-preparation knowledge/skills/information/attitudes for the 50% of the students who will seek to enter the work force immediately and/or enroll in vocational-technical institutions after high school. We cannot settle for reformation of education which affects only half of the students, but revamp of vocational-technical curricula might be a good starting point, and could serve as a model for wholesale reformation.

For example, in my own town, where less than 35% of our high school graduates go on to college, the area employers and a responsive school administration are precipitating a from-scratch design of a technical learning center to meet the needs of those students. Also we will offer learning opportunities for college-bound students, and will offer adult learning programs. The key event in my town was recognition by the employers and the educational leadership that a serious problem existed concerning this particular body of students.

Accomplishment 2: *Agreement on general purpose and goals of education*

As argued in Chapter 3, a key step in the reformation process is a community consensus on the general purpose and general goals of education. I must again emphasize the importance of this step; we must not make assumptions. The entire direction of redesign is determined by purpose and goals.

It is well worth a meeting of *all* members of the constituency just to come to an agreement on purpose and goals before any additional steps are taken. This might be accomplished by an open-to-the-public meeting, as it was in our town. Examples of constituency representatives who should be invited and encouraged to attend: heads of business/industry/government organizations; board of education; news media; school principals and curriculum directors; children services; PTA; law enforcement; judicial system; housing authority; state department of education; religious leaders; labor unions; nearby college and technical school heads; city/county commission and mayor/city manager; citizen action groups; Congresspersons; state legislators.

I believe it would be wise to start such meeting by emphasizing the key role formal education has in producing the kind of society most of the attendees are likely to want: Lawful, orderly, ethical and safe; equal opportunity for all; good economic base; productive citizenship and so forth. Then, I recommend a focus on the purpose of education. One could offer the purpose I've suggested to start the discussion: *To produce graduates who have K/S/I/A relevant to ACCOMPLISHED CITIZENSHIP.*

Given consensus on the overall purpose, I suggest moving to the development of general GOALS, consistent with the purpose such as:

- *Teach knowledge/skills/information relevant to becoming accomplished members of society.*
- *... K/S/I relevant to becoming accomplished family members.*
- *... relevant to becoming accomplished future workers.*
- *... becoming accomplished individuals.*

In this initial meeting I suggest NOT dealing in detail with the values issue. Values are always spoken about in such soft terms that nothing meaningful is likely to be produced at this first meeting. Also, the topic could raise some controversy which could polarize the constituency before it can be properly dealt with. If the values issue arises, I suggest simply saying the views of the constituency on this matter will be elicited, and that the issue will be discussed after more detailed definition and examples are produced during the first part the process.

I suggest avoiding much discussion of causes and blame for problems associated with education in this meeting. We are likely to get more cooperation if we take a positive stance.

Certainly avoid discussion of specific content and design issues. Emphasize that analysis must occur before design. We don't decide the transportation mode for trip before we decide where we are going.

Accomplishment 3: *Description of desired accomplishments, behavioral processes, and attitudes/values*

I suggest forming a steering committee headed by the superintendent, and made up of the chairs of the other functioning committees. The chair of the Board of Education should also be a member. I recommend that representatives of the group(s) who precipitated the attention to the need for reform might be on the steering panel.

It would be wise if the steering committee itself performed a general problem diagnosis as outlined in Chapter 5. The committee might need a consultant to aid them in this process.

Given the outputs of the problem-diagnosis effort, a committee to perform a needs assessment should be formed. This group should conduct the actual data collection concerning the desired student accomplishments and behavioral processes. Thus, a sub-committee for each segment of the student's life should be organized. For example, the needs assessment sub-committees might be: work preparation; family member; society member; individual.

The chair of the needs assessment committee should be a person who is accomplished at surveys and data collection, or a consultant specializing in this kind of data collection might be engaged for this purpose. (In our town I donated my time to assist the committees for this pivotal event.) Examples were given in Chapter 8.

Each committee must then implement the data collection process by some combination of written surveys, one-on-one interviews, and meetings with each segment of the constituency. The data collection effort by each sub-committee should address at least these research questions:

- What should the students be able to produce by the end of the K-12 process?
- What should they be able to do/think in order to produce each major accomplishment?
- What specific attitudes/values should they have?
- In addition to teaching knowledge/skill/information/ attitude, what additional roles should the schools play in the development of the young and improvement of the community?

Accomplishment 4: *Decisions concerning scope of reform*

Given the outputs of the work above, the steering committee should address at least these issues:

- Which major accomplishments, behavioral processes, and attitudes/values are the more frequent ones and seem to be more important to the general goals?
- Are some of the major accomplishments and behavioral processes contingent on the acquisition of the K/S/I associated with other major accomplishments?
- Does it appear there is sufficient evidence of need and community support to justify complete redesign of the entire K-12 curriculum? If not, does it appear there is sufficient need and support to redesign part of the curriculum? (For example, redesign of the curriculum for the goal regarding work preparation.)
- Does it appear that expanding the role of the school in the community is indicated? Examples: pre-natal

instruction for parents; infant and early childhood care and development instruction for parents; Head Start-type programs; after-school and weekend instructional programs; evening courses for adults; cooperation with degree-granting institutions; contact point for family and children services agencies.

- How will the various components be evaluated?
- What are the potential sources of funding for the redesign, development, and implementation? Examples: grants; local tax; private funding; re-allocation of existing resources.

Accomplishment 5: *Organization and plans for redesign*

Given the scope and parameters of the reformation effort, design teams should be formed. Examples:

- *Integration:* Committee responsible for seeing that all elements and programs are compatible and seamless.
- *Content derivation and design:* Teams for deriving the specific knowledge/skills/information/attitudes to be taught; formulating the content into courses and activities.
- *Staff selection and training:* Teams responsible for selection, assignment, and training of teachers for their new role as instructional scientists for accomplishment-based learning activities.
- *New program development:* Teams responsible for the design, development, and implementation of any new programs such as parent instruction and community services to be offered under the auspices of the school, and other programs for special situations.
- *Logistics:* Committee responsible for scheduling, space allocation, transportation, new equipment, community liaison.

Accomplishment 6: *Curriculum design*

AFTER initial training in Instructional Science and motivational methods, the teachers should then take the lead in design of the curriculum elements as outlined in Chapters 12 and 13. This might be better accomplished with the aid of a consultant or a group experienced in accomplishment-based curriculum design.

Accomplishment 7: *Decisions concerning implementation*

Given the outputs of analysis and design, at least the following major decisions are indicated:

- Will the new designs will be phased in gradually, or will a wholesale cut-over occur?
- What are the implications of the new design regarding physical facilities, instructional equipment, transportation? How will these changes/ additions, if any, be funded?
- Who will teach what?
- How will the effort be evaluated?
- Who needs to be alerted of the new design and the implications for them? For example: parents, community services, accrediting agencies, potential employers, colleges and other post-high school institutions of learning.

Again, it is important the accomplishments be produced in the sequence above. It is important that none of the outputs be omitted if we want to get to educational Eden.

How we'll know when we've arrived in
Eden

It would be overly presumptuous of me to try to dictate the results of the process outlined above. The accomplishments must be produced community by community. One size will not fit all. Some might opt for a redefinition of schooling that is all-encompassing: Design of schools such that they are the contact point for almost all activities involving learning for all ages, a life-long learning center for the community. Others might elect to confine the schoolhouse as the delivery mechanism for the traditional K-12 years; or, confined to one of the "lives" of students, such as work-preparation.

I do suggest, however, the following general principles and characteristics should be evident in the reformation of education for whatever the scope and specific design that result. That is, the probability is increased we will have an ***accomplished school*** when there is:

1. *Prime input from the constituency*
    A basic premise is that education should be "customer-driven." This means that all constituencies should have an input—parents, potential employers, the citizenry at large. The primary inputs must come from the constituencies to produce Accomplishments 1, 2, and 3—matters concerning the purpose, needs, and content of education.

    Communities change. Education must accommodate and cope with the changing needs of the society of which it is a sub-set. Thus, the provision for community inputs to content and services offered by the school must not be a one-time event, but be sought on a regular, if not continuous, basis. I see very little downside to the persons charged with curriculum development being in constant contact with parents, potential employers, and the general citizenry.

2. *Content that is accomplishment-based and integrated*
What is taught is derived out of analysis of desired outputs and relevant behavioral processes. Subject-matter-based content must be abandoned for reasons described in Chapter 6.

Content of one course is linked to content of past, current, and future courses.

3. *A curriculum designed and delivered to produce high-levels of learning*
Although there are many "if's" and "but's," it is inescapable: **If the students haven't learned, the schools haven't taught.** The best measure of instruction is by assessing degree of learning. How to produce learning to comparably high levels is generally not known to most teachers. A general outline of the elements relevant to influencing learning is presented in Chapter 13.

In order for teachers to carry out the tactics for achieving learning they must first be trained to do so. In addition, teachers and parents must carry out an effective methodology for motivating students, as outlined in Chapter 14.

4. *High and clear expectations by teachers and parents*
This is the opposite of the belief that some will achieve high levels of learning, others will fail, and most will be in the mid-range. Fairly good research seems to show that expectations (high or low) by teachers and parents tend to become reality. If so, why not aim high?

There is some evidence to support the positive effects on learning and motivation of letting the students in on WHAT is expected of them at the beginning of instructional increments. Some educators call these *objectives*. A good objective communicates to the students what they'll be able to DO at the end of instruction and what the CRITERIA are.

5. *A response to individual differences in students*
   In the design and delivery of instruction a critical characteristic must be that at least these individual differences in students are accommodated as much as practical:
   - Rate of learning
   - Entry knowledge and skills acquired prior to school
   - Previous history of success and failure ("motivation")
   - Learning style
   - Aspirations and goals
   - Interests

6. *On-going involvement of parents*
   In the accomplished schools parents go beyond the usual definition of "involvement," which is usually defined as going to PTA meetings, helping with bake sales, and being herd-drovers on school outings. Though those things might be helpful, in the accomplished school parents are co-conspirators with the teacher. Parents should:
   - Regard education as a seamless process starting in infancy not in the fifth or sixth year of the child's life.
   - Model and teach their child the values consistent with those of the accomplished citizen.
   - Read to or read with the child every day.
   - Make everyday events (shopping, banking, cooking, travel etc.) a learning opportunity.
   - Set high expectations.
   - Employ the positive approaches to motivation outlined in Chapter 14.
   - Insist on two-way communication with the teacher.
   - Insist on frequent feedback concerning their student's progress.

   In the accomplished school the parent might volunteer to teach specific modules/units of instruction in which they have specialized knowledge.

7. *High level results*

The accomplished school is one that produces students who achieve a high level of learning as measured by what they can do and accomplish as compared to the criteria for the desired performance; and, aims to produce high levels of learning in all children. Such evaluation would be more valuable to all concerned than tests of subject-matter acquisition.

A Final
WORD ...

There is an old joke about a lost traveler asking for directions of a Maine farmer. The punch line is *you can't get there from here.* In a sense, we cannot get to Eden from Medianville. We must start from a new home-BASE.

At the risk of metaphorical overkill, urban-renewal has been the usual model for educational reform. When an area of the town becomes blighted, the citizens cooperate with public and private agencies to fix-up the structures and the environment. Sometimes mere redecoration is insufficient; often massive renovation is indicated.

Redecoration or even renovation probably will not be sufficient to achieve the kind of educational system we must have. Much of the previous attempts at educational reform have been akin to repainting buildings, and occasionally rebuilding part of the structure. I, and others, are beginning to accept the painful truth we cannot just tinker with the existing the educational system, but perhaps must build it from scratch. We probably cannot convert Medianville to Eden because educational Medianville is constructed on the weak foundation of subject-matter-based instruction.

The new foundation for schools I have suggested is, the CONTENT of the K-12 curriculum that is derived systematically from a PURPOSEful, GOAL-driven, ACCOMPLISHMENT-based, BEHAVIORal analysis.

I no longer believe the stimulus for educational reform of the magnitude needed will come from inside the educational system. While I think many educators are generally altruistic and most have a genuine desire to benefit the young, their current paradigms are too well-entrenched for them to undergo more than token examination of WHAT should be taught. (Good teachers, however, are constantly vigilant concerning improving HOW it is taught and perhaps would be somewhat more receptive to Instructional Science. But why bother to continue to teach relatively low-worth content?)

I don't think the stimulus for wholesale change will arise from recognition by educators of the need to revamp education in the most fundamental of ways, but they must play an essential role in the reconstruction process.

In order to change in a dramatic way, we first need to recognize important problems exist; and, we must have knowledge of how to solve them or minimize the effects; and, we must have an incentive to develop and implement the solutions. It could be argued the traditional educational establishment does not possess any of these requirements at the present.

As I have constantly argued herein, it is the stakeholder/customer who must not only precipitate the change process, but be actively involved in the progression. The problem and the solution lie with ourselves.

BIBLIOGRAPHY

Banathy, Bela H. *Systems Design of Education*. Englewood Cliffs, New Jersey: Educational Technology Publications, 1991.

Baron, Joan Boykoff and Sternberg, Robert J. *Teaching Thinking Skills*. New York: W.H. Freeman and Company, 1987.

Barzun, Jacques *Begin Here: The Forgotten Conditions of Learning*. Chicago: University of Chicago Press, 1991.

Bennett, William J. *Our Children and Our Country: Improving America's Schools and Affirming the Common Culture*. New York: Simon and Schuster, 1988.

Binder, Carl "Behavioral Fluency: Evolution of a New Paradigm," *Behavior Analyst,* 1996.

Bloom, Allan *The Closing of the American Mind*. New York: Simon and Shuster, 1987.

Brandwein, Paul F. *Memorandum: On Renewing Schooling and Education*. New York: Harcourt Brace Jovanovich, 1981.

Bowsher, Jack E. *Educating America: Lessons Learned in the Nation's Corporations*. New York: John Wiley & Sons, 1989.

Boyer, Ernest L. *The Basic School*. Princeton, New Jersey: Carnegie Foundation for Advancement of Teaching, 1995.

Calvin, William H. *How Brains Think. New York:* Basic Books, 1996.

Carnevale, Anthony P. et al *Workplace Basics*. San Francisco: Jossey-Bass, 1990.

Collins, Marva and Tamarkin, Civia *Marva Collins' Way*. Los Angeles: Jeremy P. Tarcher, Inc., 1982.

Dean, Peter and Ripley, David E. *Performance Pathfinders*. Washington, D.C.: International Society for Performance Improvement, 1997.

de Bono, Edward *Teaching Thinking*. Harmondsworth, Middlesex, England: Penquin Books, 1976.

Dobson, James. *Dare To Discipline*. Wheaton, Illinois: Tyndale House Publishers, 1982.

Finn, Chester E. Jr. *We Must Take Charge: Our Schools and Our Future*. New York: The Free Press, 1991.

Fiske, Edward B. *Smart Kids, Smart Schools*. New York: Simon & Schuster, 1992.

Gardner, Howard *The Unschooled Mind*. New York: BasicBooks, 1991.

Gilbert, Thomas F. *Human Competence: Engineering Worthy Performance*. Amherst, Massachusettes: HRD Press, 1996.

Gerstner, Louis V. et al. *Reinventing Education*. New York: Penquin Books USA, 1995.

Glasser, William *Schools Without Failure*. New York: Harper Colophon Books, 1969.

____*The Quality School*. New York: HarperCollins, 1992.

____*The Quality School Teacher*. New York: HarperCollins, 1993.

Gross, Ronald and Beatrice (editors). *The Great School Debate*. New York: Simon& Schuster, 1985.

Hanushek, Eric et al. *Making Schools Work*. Washington, D.C.: The Brookings Institute, 1994.

Harless, Joe and Lineberry, C.S. *Turning Kids On and Off*. Newnan, Georgia: Guild V Publications,1971.

Harless, Joe *An Ounce of Analysis*. Newnan, Georgia: Guild V Publications, 1970.

____*Accomplishment-Based Curriculum Development System*. Newnan, Georgia: Guild V Publications, 1987.

____*Performance Improvement Process*. Newnan, Georgia: Guild V Publications, 1992.

Hiemstra, Roger and Sisco, Burton. *Individualizing Instruction*. San Francisco: Jossey-Bass, 1990.

Hirsch Jr., E.D. Cultural Literacy. New York: Vintage Books, 1988.

____*The Schools We Need & Why We Don't Have Them*. New York: Doubleday, 1996.

Illich, Ivan. *Deschooling Society*. New York: Harper & Rowe, 1970.

Kaufman, Roger. *Mapping Educational Success*. Newbury Park, California: Corwin Press, 1992.

Kohl, Herbert. *Basic Skills*. New York: Bantam Books, 1984.

Korn, Claire V. *Alternative American Schools*. Albany: State University of New York Press, 1991.

Levine, David et al. *Rethinking Schools*. New York: The New Press, 1995.

Luksik, Peg and Hoffecker, Pamela Hobbs. *Outcome-Based Education: The State's Assault on Our Children's Values*. Lafayette, Louisiana: Huntington House, 1995.

Mager, Robert F. *How To Turn Learners On Without Turning Them Off*. Atlanta: Center for Effective Performance, 1997.

Martz, Larry. *Making Schools Better*. New York: Times Books, 1992.

Nathan, Joe. *Charter Schools*. San Francisco: Jossey-Bass, 1996.

Postman, Neil and Weingartner. *The School Book*. New York: Delacorte Press, 1973.

Ravitch, Diane and Finn, Chester E. *What Do Our 17-Year Olds Know?* New York: Harper & Rowe, 1987.

Rogers, Carl *Freedom to Learn*. Columbus, Ohio: Charles E. Merrill Publishing, 1969.

Schlechty, Phillip C. *Schools for the Twenty-First Century*. San Francisco: Jossey-Bass, 1990.

____*Inventing Better Schools*. San Francisco: Jossey-Bass, 1997.

Sizer, Theodore R. *Horace's Compromise: The Dilemma of the American High School*. Boston: Houghton Mifflin, 1992.

Stolovitch, Harold D. and Keeps, Erica J. (Editors) *Handbook of Human Performance Technology*. San Francisco: Jossey-Bass, 1992.

Tewel, Kenneth J. *New Schools for a New Century*. Delray Beach, Florida: St. Lucie Press, 1995.

Tyack, David and Cuban, Larry. *Tinkering Toward Utopia*. Cambridge, Massachusetts: Harvard University Press, 1995.

Epilogue

The Central Educational Center Story
by Carl Binder

There have been many visionary books in the field of education. Few, however, provide step-by-step instructions for achieving the vision they describe. And even fewer ultimately produce outcomes to match their visions. *The Eden Conspiracy* is one such book, and this addendum to the new edition summarizes the significant achievements in execution of its vision that have occurred in the nearly 20 years since Joe Harless wrote this book. This is an ongoing story, to be sure. But for those readers intrigued by the potential of accomplishment-based educational design, this story is both instructive and inspiring, providing a vibrant answer to the question posed by Joe Harless, "What is the purpose of education?"

For more detailed information, see the reference list at the end of this Epilogue, with additional reading material as well as links to online video segments describing the history, rationale, and outcomes related to implementation of *The Eden Conspiracy*.

The Central Educational Center

In 2015, the Central Educational Center (CEC) in Newnan, Georgia, entered its sixteenth year of operation. CEC was the first application of the concepts and designs outlined in *The Eden Conspiracy: Educating for Accomplished Citizenship*. After more than two years of planning, CEC opened its doors in 2000 and was immediately chosen as the model for educational reform and "seamless" education in the state of Georgia. CEC has been replicated 36 times in Georgia. More than 500 groups from around the nation have visited, and there have been visits from 18 different countries.

In 2004, CEC was named one of the "30 replicable national high school reform models" by the International Center for Leadership in Education in a study funded by the Bill and Melinda Gates Foundation.

What Makes CEC Such a Desirable Model?

First, it was a grassroots movement to solve a community problem. Joe Harless and a 20-member steering committee engaged hundreds of fellow Coweta County, Georgia, citizens as well as the Coweta County School System and Carroll Tech (now West Georgia Technical College) to create a curriculum based on a needs assessment. Forty percent of the county's business and industry responded to the needs assessment, covering eighty percent of the manufacturing and trade jobs in the county. The resulting CEC curriculum combined secondary, post-secondary, and adult community education in one location, making high school and adult education "seamless." Charter school status allowed greater flexibility in developing curricula, more involvement by the community, and greater flexibility in staffing, and eliminated some bureaucracy required of other public schools. The school, by design, is led by a CEO with business and industry experience and is directed by a Governing Board with stakeholders representing the entire community. The CEO was in place for the transition from steering committee leadership to Governing Board direction.

Second, community engagement and the Analysis, Design, Development, Implementation, and Evaluation approach (ADDIE) to systemic change in education that generated CEC's creation are continued today in the governing structure. This structure allows the organization to continually monitor the ever-changing needs of the workforce in the county, and to be locally controlled.

In the 36 replications of CEC in Georgia, each is locally controlled. There is state support without the burden of state bureaucracy. Historically, all the replications have followed CEC example of local funding, with the state only contributing funds "for the last mile." When Georgia Governor Roy Barnes signed the budget appropriating $7 million to construct two technology wings for the original school in April of 2000, CEC was up and running, having invested more than two years of planning and more than $10 million of local money.

The third and critical factor making CEC a desirable model is its dependence on partnerships in the community. These partnerships allow CEC to design hands-on, real-world experiences in courses tailored to local workforce needs. Partners like the Cancer Treatment Centers of America provide opportunities for internships. CEC students dual-enrolled in West Georgia Technical College and its culinary arts program cater events in the community. Local manufacturers, some of whom have established or expanded their facilities as a direct result of CEC's ability to produce skilled employees, provide workplace learning experiences coordinated with students' high school schedules and courses offered by the College.

The Coweta Samaritan Clinic, through its dental services, and NuLink, a fiber optic company, provide experiences. The Coweta Samaritan Clinic, serving uninsured and under-served members of the community, located its new dental clinic on the CEC campus in the CEC dental lab. CEC adult and high school students who are studying to earn their collegiate dental assisting certificates volunteer alongside the area's volunteer dentists to treat patients whose health is undermined by lack of dental care. NuLink, the local cable company, merged its video production facilities with CEC and now has two television stations on the campus. Students in the Broadcast Video II class work hands-on with video broadcasting and have their productions aired on local television. Students can expand their work experience further with Georgia Public Television internships.

In a February 6, 2000, interview in *The Times-Herald* (Newnan, Georgia) discussing the book *The Eden Conspiracy*, Joe Harless was asked if the Central Educational Center was a fair test of his theories. "The answer was yes and no. 'Central will be a good test of these concepts, but will fall short of what my dream is, because we have had to make practical compromises.' And because the CEC focuses largely on technical education, while Harless wants to see his theories carried over into schools in general."

Nonetheless, because of its foundation in community-wide stakeholder engagement and analysis, and its focus on the accomplishments that students must produce to achieve high-paying employment and successful citizenship, CEC points the way to a new model for educational reform: bottom-up rather than top-down. Moreover, to the extent that evidence-based instructional designers and program developers continue to pursue Harless's vision of the accomplished citizen, the potential for continuous improvement toward broader realization of that vision is enormous.

The Economic and Social Impact of CEC

CEC had an opportunity for enormous impact on the economy before it even opened its doors. The Newnan division of Yamaha Motor Manufacturing Corporation was being directed by its Japanese ownership to increase its manufacturing base with new products and automated processes. Various states and communities across the United States were offering tax credits in exchange for relocation. Traditionally, Coweta County did not offer tax credits. What Yamaha preferred to tax credits was what CEC could offer: a pipeline of young people who have the skill set and the work ethic to enter the work of automation and manufacturing. Because of CEC's structure, it could respond to that need. There were curriculum changes, and Yamaha outfitted an engineering lab. Yamaha spent $40 million to build new facilities in Newnan and added 300 new jobs. Since that decision, Yamaha has continued to expand to become the largest private employer in Coweta County.

CEC had a part in recruiting the Cancer Treatment Centers of America (CTCA) for Newnan. CTCA began its search with a list of 40 potential locations. When the final list was narrowed to three sites, all were in Georgia. All had College and Career Academies (the Georgia name for CEC replications). CTCA projected that in the first five years there would be 500 employees and $500 million in economic impact. After the first three years, there were 900 employees and a probable impact of over $1 billion dollars, according to reports from the company and local economic development authorities.

CEC played a role in assisting the community to attract Piedmont Healthcare, traditionally one of Georgia's most highly rated healthcare providers, to purchase the local community hospital. Piedmont has spent more than $150 million to build a state-of-the-art replacement hospital facility, has expanded local services, and continues to hire healthcare workforce. The largest single number of CEC interns works with Piedmont-Newnan Hospital.

Many CEC students are dual-enrolled with West Georgia Technical College in certificate granting programs designed by employers, the college, and the state. The local Economic Development Authority uses the number of dual enrollment certificates achieved as a recruiting tool when multi-national corporations are being lured to the community. The dual enrollment certificates were among the incentives used in locating Niagara Bottling in Coweta County. Niagara is touted as the most automated water bottling facility in the world.

The president of the Coweta County Development Authority, Greg Wright, recently wrote in *The Newnan Times-Herald* Chamber of Commerce insert, "There are countless examples of how the CEC is having a positive impact on the lives of our future workforce, but there are also countless examples of how CEC is helping our existing community of businesses and industries grow and succeed. Synergies like those in place at CEC are the types of partnerships that have helped our community grow jobs at a level four times higher than the state average." Given current-day challenges of a shrinking middle class and growing income inequality, a proven model that prepares young people for high-wage, high-skilled jobs is quite timely.

Before CEC, there was no technical college in Coweta County. Students drove 25 miles to neighboring Carroll Tech (now West Georgia Technical College). At the inception of CEC, it partnered with Carroll Tech to bring classes to the CEC campus in Newnan that fit the specific needs identified in the stakeholder analysis for Coweta County. CEC takes pride in having staged the next level of growth for Carroll Tech. Carroll Tech has uptiered to become West Georgia Technical College (WGTC) offering an associate's degree that may transfer to a university. West Georgia Technical

College is now the third largest of 22 accredited public technical colleges across Georgia.

Currently CEC is working with the German American Chambers of Commerce and the State of Georgia, to develop the first real, three-year, "German" apprenticeships in Georgia. The curriculum for apprenticeship is the national curriculum approved by the German Chamber and companies across Germany and the business partner in Coweta County with German corporate ownership. Students will gain both post-secondary credentials and German national certification recognized worldwide. The program officially launched in 2016.

The impact on individual and family income has also been significant. As an example, in 2014, 55 graduates simultaneously received high school diplomas and college welding certificates. This gave them the opportunity to work in many manufacturing jobs in Coweta County that pay an average of $23 an hour, compared with the median U.S. wage of $13.25 per hour reported by the Bureau of Labor Statistics in 2014. This can provide a significant jump-up in income for an 18-year-old, whether continuing on to a college bachelor's program or taking a full-time job after graduation.

This model provides a reliable path for young people to climb the ladder of social and economic mobility, sorely needed in this age of growing economic inequality in America.

Examples of Individual Students

As with any group of students, there are exceptional ones at CEC. But interviews and informal conversations with students in the spring of 2016 revealed an unusual degree of enthusiasm, engagement, and achievement among a large number of the students.

The degree of engagement in CEC students seems exceptional, in contrast with typical groups in high schools who often seem distracted and cynical. In classes with adults completing programs in the Technical College, and at workplace learning sites, one high school-age student mentioned that "[I] feel like me, the real me, unlike at high school where I felt like a kid."

One young lady in the video production program, who works in front of the camera as "talent," described her experience as an intern at Georgia Public Television. Professionally dressed, even during her CEC classes, she described her surprise to find college educated interns not making eye contact, not "acting or dressing professionally," and generally not up to the standards of workplace behavior that she had learned at CEC. At 17, she was offered a full time job at GPTV, which she was deciding whether to accept when we spoke.

A young man, who was first turned on to robotics in a course run by a long-time manufacturing professional at CEC, went on to a college program at Georgia Tech and was planning to apply to MIT's Media Lab upon graduation from college.

Another young woman was excited to learn that she and her project partners had won a National Student Production Award (the high school "Emmy") for a video segment, and was invited to participate in a national competition in New York. CEC Broadcast Video students, for the past two years, have earned more High School Production (Emmy) Awards than any other southeastern U. S. program.

While these cases might be exceptional in some respects, observations and interviews with many other students revealed a level of accomplishment, personal maturity, and enthusiasm seldom seen in typical high school students. These young people are on paths toward the rest of their lives, having early opportunities to sample possible career paths, decide for or against those paths, and pursue their interests in ways that lead to real world achievements and success.

Bipartisan Appeal of CEC

Both Democrats and Republicans found it easy to endorse the model set up by the CEC steering committee: work within the system, secure status as a charter school, work in partnership with business and educators, and work backward from the post-school world to determine what should be taught. Governor Roy Barnes (Democrat) pushed for funding technology wings for a heavily Republican district. He saw CEC as a model for educational reform in the state of Georgia.

Political and community leaders alike boast: "Students can graduate from high school on Friday night, graduate from technical college on Saturday night, and go to work on Monday in a job that is waiting for them." (In many cases, the student also earns industry certification.)

Politicians and business leaders alike point out that dual enrollment creates a more highly skilled high school graduate. They have found that the CEC graduates will earn twice as much as those with only a high school diploma. In addition, dual enrollment makes educational expenditures more efficient.

The present Lieutenant Governor of Georgia, Casey Cagle, was a Republican State Senator on Governor Barnes's Education Reform Study Commission. The commission recommended to Governor Barnes that CEC be chosen as the educational reform model for the state. In 2006, Cagle was elected Georgia's first Republican Lt. Governor. He campaigned tirelessly for charter school systems and College and Career Academies (with CEC as the model) in his legislative years and in his Lt. Governor campaigns. In his 2014 campaign, he made headlines as he visited College and Career Academies across the state. His TV ads featured these visits, and he has published a book of his own promoting an educational philosophy that closely aligns with key elements of Harless's vision.

Former Superintendent of Schools for Coweta County Richard Brooks attributed CEC's success to the fact that people throughout the community "forged a common vision that was greater than ourselves." (*The Times-Herald,* January 31, 2002) A powerful ramification of the whole-community stakeholder analysis driven by Harless's methodology is that programs and systems adopted after deep engagement by stakeholders from all parts of a community are more likely to sustain themselves than programs imposed top-down by educational experts or policy makers.

It is this bottom-up aspect of Harless's approach that seems most promising for the future of educational reform, which has over the decades failed in so many efforts around the nation when key top-down influencers and leaders have left or been removed from those efforts. A community-driven effort is simply more likely to succeed, in part because it provides stakeholders in all segments with greater rewards produced by programs or systems that they design based on the accomplishments they need. The system, in that regard, is more likely to be self-reinforcing, thus self-sustaining.

Cultural Significance

From a cultural perspective, the accomplishment-based approach advocated by *The Eden Conspiracy*, and embodied in CEC addresses an underlying issue that some (e.g., Pennypacker, 1973) have described as the "problem" with adolescence in current day society. Unlike traditional societies, modern culture tends to isolate adolescents from the responsibilities of adulthood in a way that unnecessarily disconnects them from the accomplishments they will need to succeed as adults. Lacking requirements for self-support and what might be called an "adult apprenticeship" period seen in more traditional cultures, in which adolescents begin to learn how to accomplish what will be needed for gainful employment and self-support, family life, and active participation in community, today's adolescents often waste time, get into trouble, and develop habits that do not advance their maturity.

In contrast, CEC students as young as 14 are energized by their participation in activities directed toward careers of their choice and mature participation in society. The accomplishments they are learning how to produce during this period are those that they will need as adults. Their excitement about following a direct path from school to careers and into lives of their choice is palpable, even in the halls and in casual conversations. These students are anything but "lost" in the teenage years. Instead, they are engaged, excited, and productive as they look toward a seamless progression into adulthood.

CEC Today

Today the plant and equipment at CEC are valued at approximately $30 million, but the partnerships that forged the school and continue to keep it connected to the community are ultimately worth much more to the citizens of Coweta County.

Replications across Georgia are in various stages of development, and not all have modeled CEC in every respect. However, their grounding in an accomplishment-based analysis that includes all stakeholders in the community, following Harless's model, make them integral, even organic elements of the communities they serve.

International replication is a particularly interesting development for CEC. In addition to the German Apprenticeship program recently begun in Coweta County in partnership with CEC, replications of the model in India and other nations are emerging. This model, with its focus on stakeholder-identified accomplishments, is robust and adaptable for a wide range of different cultural and economic environments.

Even at CEC, Harless's systematic approach to instructional design anchored in target accomplishments is not practiced with the rigor he intended. However, because these programs are adaptive and responsive to community needs, they are outcome-oriented and tend toward more effective rather than less effective instructional designs. There is openness to continuous improvement and expansion, which may include more systematic application of instructional science, as well as extensions of the accomplishment-based model into educational programs other than College and Career Academies.

In any case, the power of shifting program design from subject matter to needed accomplishments for work life and citizenry is impressive. As one colleague of ours in the organizational performance improvement field is fond of saying, "Accomplishments liberate behavior." What is evident at CEC and in its replications is that by defining desired accomplishments, we allow flexibility in the behavior needed to produce them, and in the curriculum and instructional methods for ensuring that students can produce those accomplishments. The concreteness and real world relevance of an accomplishment-based approach makes this model self-improving.

Key Take-Aways

CEC and its ongoing replications provide important insights for the future of education and educational reform, including:

- An accomplishment-based approach to curriculum design is inherently superior to one based on categories of subject matter, or even behavioral objectives, because at every level students are producing valuable products aligned with their own goals and purpose.
- Participation in the analysis, design, and governance of educational programs by stakeholders representing all segments of a community provides a more certain path to sustainment and continuous improvement than a more conventional top-down approach to educational reform, with guidelines and design imposed "from above" by experts or policy makers.
- Focusing on the needs of the local employment community anchors the program in goals and objectives that will have long-term value for individuals, the community, and the society at large. Continuous refinement and revision, based on changing needs, ensures enduring value and sustainment.
- In addition to a focus on specific employment and citizen accomplishments, explicitly including elements related to "work ethic" and mature social conduct ensures that graduates can transition into full time employment and community involvement, or further education, once they graduate from the program.

For More Information

CEC in Newnan, Georgia, welcomes visitors and encourages interest. CEC students routinely create and publish video material from their professional studios/classrooms on the Internet, and seek out professional interest in opportunities for improvement. With political and economic support from all levels in the state, this model is sure to continue and expand over the coming years. And for those interested in combining an even more rigorous approach to curriculum and instruction with the accomplishment-based methodology presented in this book, opportunities for improvement and replication seem unlimited.

Many Thanks to the CEO of CEC

Mark Whitlock, after a successful career in international banking for Bank of America, returned to Newnan, Georgia, his place of origin, to serve as founding CEO of the Central Educational Center. He, along with the local Economic Development Office and the *The Newnan Times-Herald*, has archived the accomplishments of CEC. Mark has provided vital information for the Introduction and Epilogue through an onsite visit and countless interviews. As the CEO of CEC, Mark has a unique leadership role in his community and in education in the State of Georgia. He has forged the partnerships with business and industry that provide learning and career opportunities for his students. Through his coaching and leadership, the replications of CEC throughout Georgia have had support and guidance. His exemplary recruiting of faculty from the best of their professions has taken full advantage of flexibility in staffing under Georgia charter school guidelines. It is hard to imagine what the CEC effort would have yielded without his full implementation of the unique CEO role.

References

Chow, A. (2008). *Systems Thinking and 21st Century Education: A Case Study of an American Model for High School Educational Reform.* Germany: VDM Verlag Dr. Muller Aktiengestellschaft & Co. KG. Publication of a Florida State University doctoral dissertation provides detailed background and analysis of Harless's model and its implementation in the Central Educational Center.

Pennypacker, H.S. (1973). *The Challenge of Youth.* In R. Ulrich, T. Stachnik, and W. Mabry (Eds.), <u>Control of Human Behavior Volume Three.</u> New York: Scott Foresman, 432-436.

Selected Web Links and Videos

Central Educational Center web site:
www.centraleducationalcenter.net

Introduction to CEC as a Joint Venture by Mark Whitlock,
CEO: http://newnanceo.com/video/2016/06/mark-whitlock-
central-educational-center-and-chamber-partnership/

School Spotlight–Central Educational Center: https://www.
youtube.com/watch?v=-4GbN9mwVFA

The CEC Times (an online student publication):
http://cectimes.com

"Hire Education": A Vocational Model Succeeds – CNN Coverage
of CEC: http://www.cnn.com/2007/EDUCATION/03/07/cec.
career.tech/index.html?iref=newssearch

Lt. Governor Casey Cagle on the CEC German apprenticeship
program: http://times-herald.com/news/2016/05/cagle-kicks-
off-german-style-apprenticeship-program

College and Career Academy Student Spotlight–Julie
Lenderman: https://ltgov.georgia.gov/college-and-career-
academy-student-spotlight-julie-lenderman

Carl Binder, CPT, PhD, is President of the Performance Thinking Network (www.SixBoxes.com) and has been helping client organizations worldwide improve performance with research-based methods for over 35 years. After studying with B.F. Skinner as a doctoral student in Experimental Psychology at Harvard, he spent several decades conducting instructional research, developing curriculum, and training teachers. These pursuits overlapped with his work in organizational performance improvement that began during the 1980's. He has had many mentors in his career, and Joe Harless was one of the most important, along with Beatrice Barrett, Eric Haughton, Ogden Lindsley, Tom Gilbert, and Robert Horn. Carl has published roughly 60 professional articles and chapters, and has been honored with lifetime achievement awards from the American Psychological Association (APA), the International Society for Performance Improvement (ISPI), and the Organizational Behavior Management (OBM) Network. Contact Carl at carlbinder@sixboxes.com.

CAMBRIDGE CENTER
———— *FOR* ————
BEHAVIORAL STUDIES

To order
additional copies of
The Eden Conspiracy
and other
inspirational and informative
publications about
behavior science and its
applications,
visit the
CCBS Online Store
at
behavior.org

550 Newtown Road, Suite 950 • Littleton, Massachusetts 01460
Tel: (866) 509-0467 • (978) 369-2227
E-mail: center@behavior.org

CAMBRIDGE CENTER
FOR
BEHAVIORAL STUDIES

To order
additional copies of
The Eden Conspiracy
and other
inspirational and informative
publications about
behavior science and its
applications,
visit the
CCBS Online Store
at
behavior.org

550 Newtown Road, Suite 950 • Littleton, Massachusetts 01460
Tel: (866) 509-0467 • (978) 369-2227
E-mail: center@behavior.org

CPSIA information can be obtained
at www.ICGtesting.com
Printed in the USA
LVHW080337020820
662082LV00005B/27

9 781881 317180